# *God Given Right:*
## A CHILD PROTECTION STORY

BY

EMMANUEL GOMEZ

**PUBLISHED BY:**
**Emmanuel Gomez © 2010 Copyright**

Vindicate me, O God,
and plead my case against an
ungodly nation;
Rescue me from deceitful and
wicked men. –PSALMS 43:1

# CONTENTS

Have you ever lost a loved one? Imagine losing your child...
To the government.

*God Given Right*

# ONE

My wife and I made a beautiful baby girl, born April 8th, 2008. Izabela... A blessing sent to us from God. If you've ever wanted and waited for a special gift that was specially wrapped, and tempted you every chance you saw it to open it... then you might understand the anticipation that me and my wife felt. We anxiously and happily waited to see what God was sending us. The first 3-D ultra sound was the closest "hint" we acquired before actually getting to see the actual gift... A precious gift.

My wife due to pre-eclampsia was forced to have a C-section or face her chances with death. And possibly lose a most loved and cherished baby in her womb. The situation was frightening and literally death-defying. I rushed to the hospital only to be 15 minutes too late... 3 pounds 13 ounces, a beautiful baby girl. My wife was recovering, but her blood pressure was still through the roof. She had gone into labor with a blood pressure of 190. I made my way through personnel, nurses, and doctors to reach her side. I was worried for her health and didn't want to embrace the thought of losing her... I couldn't. Thank God she was ok, and only experiencing the numbness and nausea of the medications. Her pain was dulled for the moment. And our daughter was finally here, an early arrival but very happily welcome.

The maternity ward is supposed to be a place of joy, love, the welcoming of new life, and addition to the family. This process should be as pleasant and inviting as possible. A happy experience... But this was not our case. The hospital staff had turned a birthday party, and a moment of congratulations into a complete intrusion of hospital territory and the hospital's routine work shift. I was asked to leave at exactly 8:59 pm, "visiting hours are OVER" I'm told. Now take in mind, my wife is recovering from her C-section, and my daughter is being observed for any complications. She is being determined where to be sent for further treatment, since she is premature and requires a neo-natal specialist. And I am being asked to leave by a medical assistant. I don't believe they teach common sense and human decency at her medical school or nursing program, but I'm just taking a long shot here... people make normal mistakes and I didn't want to let a small disrespectful gesture protrude in the matter at hand. The doctor politely steps in on my behalf, and I am allowed to remain by my wife's side. My wife and I decided it would be best to have my daughter sent to Children's Hospital, a well recognized hospital with respected doctors in the neo-natal field. My wife would remain at the current hospital and be further observed until her blood pressure could be properly stabilized. Mother and daughter would be separated by 20 miles. "Daddy" would go and make sure our daughter was safe and being well taken care of in her absence.

# TWO

DAY TWO... JUGGLING BETWEEN, BEING A FATHER AND BEING A HUSBAND. SIMULTANEOUSLY AND IN TWO DIFFERENT LOCATIONS. BOTH THE GIRLS OF MY LIFE ARE IN THE HOSPITAL AND I WANT TO BE THERE FOR THE BOTH OF THEM. I'M TORN BETWEEN THE TWO, SO I SACRIFICE MYSELF AND ATTEND TO THE BOTH OF THEM AS BEST AS I CAN, TO THE BEST OF MY CAPABILITIES. I AM NOT FORTUNATE ENOUGH TO AFFORD A VEHICLE, AND SO I RELY ON PUBLIC TRANSPORTATION (AC TRANSIT AND BART FOR THOSE IN THE KNOW). SO I MAKE MY WAY ACROSS TOWN, AND LEAVE MY DAUGHTER'S SIDE TO GO AND GET HER A BOTTLE OF "MAMA'S FINEST" BREAST MILK (HOME BREWED AND SPECIAL BLEND). I GET TO MY WIFE'S SIDE ONLY TO FIND HER WEAK AND FEELING SORE. I WATCH HER EYES CONFESS THE PAIN SHE'S IN, AND THE DESIRE TO BE WITH OUR DAUGHTER... OUR PRECIOUS DAUGHTER. I TRY TO CONSOLE HER AND EXPLAIN TO HER HOW OUR DAUGHTER WAS BEING CARED FOR, AND BROUGHT CALM TO ALL HER DOUBTS. I TELL HER THAT THE BABY LOOKS JUST LIKE HER, AND THAT SHE'S THE CUTEST BABY... AND SMART LIKE HER DADDY. THIS BRINGS A SMILE TO HER FACE AND COMFORT TO HER HEART. I ASK HER WHAT THE DOCTORS HAVE TOLD HER ABOUT HER CONDITION, AND ASK HER HOW THEY HAVE BEEN TREATING HER. SHE RESPONDS THE SAME AS ANY CHILD WOULD EXPLAIN ALGEBRA, SHE HONESTLY DIDN'T UNDERSTAND WHAT THE DOCTOR'S REPORT MEANT. SO SHE CAN ONLY TELL ME THAT THEY TOLD HER THAT SHE COULD GO HOME IN A FEW DAYS. SHE THEN WOULD BE ABLE TO VISIT THE HOSPITAL WHERE OUR DAUGHTER WAS STAYING. SHE ALSO TELLS ME THAT THE NURSES HAVE BEEN RUDE to her, and that they don't understand the amount of pain she's in... The way they talk to her to do things that she can't do, makes her upset and causes her more pain. This made me feel terrible for her. I couldn't believe the un-compassion in the hospital staff. It was the second incident since we'd been there, where they showed disregard and lack of respect. So I asked at the front desk to speak to a manager, and requested a grievance form (conveniently there was no such form). So I had to make my grievance verbally to a staff manager that took my complaint as a joke, and actually suggested that my wife and I might have initiated the rude remarks and behavior of their staff... So now I was left reconsidering my decision of choosing this hospital in the first place, and decided I had made a horrible mistake. I couldn't believe it was possible to make a birth such an ugly experience for two new and happy parents. I was disgusted with the hospital and their staff, and I was sure to God thankful that I was not paying a dime or nickel for this treatment (a special thanks to Medi-Cal). I then was asked to leave at 9-pm on the dot, the finger hand actually struck nine when I looked up, as the nurse told me "visiting hours are OVER"... Could the air turn any staler? The stench from the hospital became nauseating.

145 over 90... My wife's blood pressure had surely improved, but not to the point where it was stable. But to my amazement and disbelief the doctor felt she was ready to go home. Now this is my personal opinion and observation, but doctors are human beings who study charts and follow other doctor's established methods of treating patients, rather then treating the patient on an individual basis themselves, and specifically to that person. So instead of actually studying the patient and seeing that she's not well yet, her routine method of 3 days post labor and then go home method will suffice... Which, it didn't. I had to rush my wife to the ER two days later with a blood pressure of 199! She

OBVIOUSLY HADN'T BECOME STABLE YET AND THE MEDICINE SHE WAS PRESCRIBED DID NOT PROCURE THE RESULTS SHE NEEDED, NOR WHAT THE GOOD DOCTOR ORDERED. WE LEFT THE ER THAT NIGHT AFTER SHE RECEIVED A DOSE OF MEDICINE INJECTED INTO HER BLOOD STREAM, AND HER BLOOD PRESSURE CAME DOWN TO 130 OR SO. WHICH, IS MORE WITHIN NORMAL LIMITS. I WATCHED HER MEDICINE DOSE SCHEDULE FROM THEN ON WITH MORE CAUTION, AND DECIDED TO DISREGARD MEDICAL ROUTINE RECOMMENDATIONS, AND GAVE HER A DOSE EVERY 6 HOURS INSTEAD OF EVERY 8 HOURS. WHICH MEANT 4 PILLS A DAY INSTEAD OF 3... PROBLEM SOLVED.

# THREE

THE VISITOR LOUNGE FOR NEO-NATAL AND ICU IS A PLACE THAT IS GENERALLY CROWDED AND FILLED WITH WORRY. NOT THE GREATEST PLACE TO BE, NOR MUCH LESS THE PERFECT HANGOUT. TO OUR LUCK IT WAS INTENDED TO ACCOMMODATE PARENTS WHO CHOSE TO STAY OVER NIGHT WITH THEIR CHILD. SO A STIFF LEATHER PULL OUT CHAIR WOULD BE OUR PLACE OF REST FOR THE NEXT FEW NIGHTS, OR UNTIL OUR DAUGHTER WAS READY TO LEAVE... STIFF NECKS AND SORE BACKS WAS WHAT WE WOKE UP TO EVERY MORNING, NOT TO MENTION THE HEADACHES THAT ARE CAUSED BY POOR SLEEP, WHEN FORCED TO SLEEP IN A NOISY AND BRIGHT ENVIRONMENT... NOT THE GREATEST FEELING. UNTIL THE MORNING WHEN WE WERE RUDELY AWAKENED BY THE HEAVY SHOUT OF A 6 FOOT 2, 230 POUND MAN SHOUTING "EVERYBODY GET UP! WAKE UP! THIS ISN'T A HOTEL." NOW YOU TELL ME... I'M IN A PARENT LOUNGE, DESIGNATED FOR PARENTS WHO HAVE A CHILD IN EITHER ICU OR THE NEO-NATAL UNIT. BOTH OF WHICH ARE SERIOUS MATTERS AND PAINFUL FOR THE FAMILIES. THE FACT OF THE VISITOR LOUNGE BEING UNCOMFORTABLE TO ADD, DOESN'T JUSTIFY THE ANGUISH OF WHAT EVERYONE IN THE ROOM IS FEELING. AND THEN TO BE WOKEN UP BY A SECURITY GUARD AT 6:40 AM! NOW I'M NOT A MORNING PERSON, AND A BIT GRUMPY IN THE MORNINGS IF YOU ASK MY WIFE, BUT THIS WAS RIDICULOUS! I WAS OUTRAGED, AND I TOLD HIM TO STOP YELLING. HE QUICKLY RESPONDED WITH, "GET YOUR BUTT UP, THIS AIN'T A PLACE TO SLEEP, GO SLEEP IN YOUR OWN HOME." NOW I'M NOT SURE IF HIS IGNORANCE TO WHERE HE WAS, OR MAYBE JUST THE FACT THAT HE HAS A JOB HAD

GONE TO HIS HEAD, BUT HE OBVIOUSLY HAD NO SENSE OF REASONING... BUT I COULD BE WRONG. EITHER WAY I TRIED TO REASON WITH HIM, AND EXPLAINED THAT I WAS A PARENT, AND THAT I HAD BEEN TOLD BY MY SOCIAL WORKER (DESIGNATED BY THE HOSPITAL) THAT WE WERE WELCOME TO SLEEP IN THAT AREA. SINCE WE LIVE ABOUT 30 MILES AWAY, AND TRANSPORTATION WAS A DIFFICULTY GETTING TO AND FROM THE HOSPITAL. HE STORMED OUT OF THE DESIGNATED AREA AND SWORE TO GET MY ATTITUDE TAKEN CARE OF, HE WOULD SPEAK TO MY SOCIAL WORKER ABOUT MY NOT WANTING TO OBEY HIS ORDERS TO GET "MY BUTT UP" (AS HE PUT IT). THIS WAS GOING TO BE A LONG AND BUMPY RIDE, I COULD SMELL THAT STALE STENCH IN THE AIR AGAIN, ONLY THIS TIME I WAS SORE AND EXTREMELY TIRED.

*RING RING* A MEETING WAS CALLED AND WE WERE TOLD IT WOULD BE A MEETING TO DISCUSS GOALS FOR OUR DAUGHTER BEING DISCHARGED, AND THAT IT WAS URGENT. (SINCE THERE HAD ALSO BEEN CONCERNS FOR ISSUES REGARDING ACCOMMODATION, OR THE "SLEEPING INCIDENT".) WHEN WE ARRIVED, WE WERE BROUGHT TO A SPECIAL ROOM, DESIGNATED FOR MEETINGS. A LARGE TABLE WITH CHAIRS ALL AROUND IT STOOD IN THE MIDDLE. WE SAT WITH THE HOSPITAL SOCIAL WORKER, A CHARGE NURSE, AND THE HEAD OF SECURITY. I WAS A BIT SURPRISED AT THE INTIMIDATION TACTICS THAT THE HEAD OF SECURITY PERVADED, AND ATTEMPTED ON ME. IT WAS A BIT HUMOROUS... SOME PEOPLE TAKE THEIR JOBS A BIT TOO SERIOUS. HONESTLY. SO HE EXPLAINS TO ME THAT HE WILL NOT TOLERATE ANY DISRESPECT TO HIS STAFF, AND THAT I WILL BE BANNED FROM THE HOSPITAL IF I DO NOT FOLLOW HIS ORDERS... I GENTLY APPROACH THE SITUATION, AS BEST AS POSSIBLE, BEING THAT I AM BEING TAUNTED, PROVOKED, AND PUSHED TO FEEL INFERIOR TO THIS HARDENED, OVER-WEIGHT MAN. I EXPLAIN THAT MY SOCIAL WORKER (WHICH IS SITTING IN THE SAME ROOM AND HASN'T UTTERED A WORD) HAD EXPLAINED TO ME THAT I COULD STAY OVER NIGHT, AND THAT I COULD SLEEP IN THE PARENT VISITOR LOUNGE. I EXPLAINED HOW HIS STAFF WAS VERY DISRESPECTFUL IN THE WAY HE APPROACHED THE SITUATION BY YELLING, AND THAT IT WAS UN-CALLED FOR. BUT I WAS PRACTICALLY SPEAKING TO MYSELF, BECAUSE ALL HE COULD reply was, "Are you going to follow the rules?" I guess I was being ignorant, or maybe I was just being misled and set for failure. Because for the life of me, I had no clue of what he was talking about. He explained that I had to be up by 6 in the morning, and that it was the rules for the lounge... I could have sworn it wasn't in my parent handbook, or even posted on the visitor walls, nor much less explained to me by our social worker. I turn to her and asked her if this was true. She said she hadn't known that these were the rules, but that since now this "fine" gentleman was stating that they were, that I had to agree to follow them or that I would be banned from visiting the hospital... For the love of God, someone tell me, am I losing my mind? Am I the bad guy in this scenario? Did I forget my code of conduct, or did I land on crapville island? A place where doctors and nurses have their own set of rules and bylaws, to which the outside world has no knowledge, understanding, or even the privilege to be a part of... For the love of God. So basically I must wake up by 6-am, or be forced to not be welcome to even visit my child that is in a serious life threatening condition? And still have to pay for the services of this un-sympathetic hospital... Bless your heart Medi-Cal.

# FOUR

For weeks I hadn't seen my daughter. I chose to never spend another night in that hospital, for fear of being banned. I had decided to not be in that negative atmosphere if even for just a visit. We prayed our daughter would be able to come home soon, and would call frequently to see about her progress. My wife would call every night and throughout the day to check on her. I would speak to her doctors to get a better understanding of her health and her treatment. It wasn't looking good... The doctors were baffled and didn't know what to do. She wasn't holding down her feedings, and was not gaining sufficient weight compared to their "blessed" chart. I'm no doctor but I know the difference between being force fed and meal time. They over fed her and apparently busted her abdomen. Imagine how a parent might feel, when you watch people do their way with your child and they harm them. It does not justify it regardless of where you went to school, how long you went to school, where you work, nor how much salary you make a year... Failure is failure and we are all human beings regardless. So I was very upset and not pleased with her treatment. Even the fact that they caused for her to reflux her feedings, and then gave her medicines to reduce the discomfort of the reflux, and yet they never even consulted with us to ask if that was ok... or explain why. We were basically not Izabela's parents in their minds, or they just didn't care that we were... Point blank. A few days later we were told she would be coming home soon, and we were relieved and excited. It was as if we were expecting her to be born once again. We were so anxious, that we began to call more frequent then usual to see about her progress, which would ultimately determine if she was going to be coming home that weekend. Just 2 exams and a study, and they would determine our fate. The last day of the study, I called and asked to speak to her nurse to find out the outcome of the study... *Click*. Someone had hung up on me, so I redialed... I asked to speak to my daughters nurse, and asked for the nurse's name that answered my call. Since she had hung up on me... *Click*. Hung up again... What's going on? I called again, but this time I wanted to speak to a charge nurse... *Click*. Are you kidding me? Redial... "Can I speak to a charge nurse?" And this was what I heard, "If you call here again you're going to be in big trouble mister, you're going to go to jail! If you threaten me again I'm going to call the police!" *Click*. Whoa... Is this really happening? And if so, why is this happening? I needed to report this person to her supervisor. This wasn't right for one, and secondly I just wanted to know how my daughter was doing. I didn't even visit her anymore to avoid any drama. And now even over the phone I was being disrespected like this? And made to seem as if I was doing something that I wasn't... Is that even legal? Because I know that it isn't professional. I don't own a business, but I'm sure if I was a boss of a major business, where a paying customer is being hung up on and being talked to in the form that the woman was talking to me, it would definitely cause for disciplinary action. But this was not the case. I was actually banned from the hospital... The reason for which I was no longer allowed in the hospital, was because they claimed that I was not complying with their rules and wasn't treating staff with respect. But that was what they said, that was in no way the truth... But I'm in Crapville Island, who cares what I have to say about anything. The secretary told her supervisor that I was making threatening remarks towards her, and that I was being very rude. So when I made it to the hospital to make my complaint in person concerning the receptionist's rude conduct, I wasn't allowed passed the front desk. I was banned from the hospital over "supposed" rude and disrespectful behavior over the phone. My only option now was to have my daughter transferred to a different hospital. I couldn't allow this kind of treatment from anyone, and I wasn't going to stand by and allow them to take away my right to be with my daughter. So I decided to tell them in my defense, that I no longer wanted my daughter treated at their hospital, and didn't feel it was in my family's best interest. And this was where all hell broke loose... Ring the alarm.

# *FIVE*

Child Protective Services... An entity entirely to itself, and for itself. It's to say, that this agency and organization tends to taking kids from parents (which constitutes as kidnapping or child abduction) with no regards for human rights, the law, nor the moral principles of respect for life and the privacy of others. Much less a respect for God, who made marriage and intended for it to be holy and between man and woman. The purpose, for which, to become as one and procreate in this process. This CPS organization was never included in God's plan, and it is clear to see why (for those in the know). Yet our local social workers with a few years of schooling are given a position with a level of power so high, that it goes to their head... Point blank. They can take away anyone's kid. If thfy have the slightest advantage, or pretext to attack and be effective, then they have themselves a paid bonus, and a raise in salary in the very near future. Along with broken families, destroyed homes, and ruined lives. (That's enough to give satan a hard-on.) Their prime target is the frequent minorities and poverty stricken families that don't have the means or the voice to defend themselves, which makes them an easy target. I catch myself in their cross-hairs, and I am in for a big treat. Now, what I have gone through has been your worst case of bad luck, crappy situations, and poor work ethics... But the thought that this was enough to intervene in my family, and take away my daughter is absurd. I am actually a little humored by the completely rude and ignorant gesture. That it has entertained me enough to believe that anyone could be so vindictive and evil, as to want to take away my child from me and my wife... So I agreed to meet with the social worker with Child Protective Services, who had called me to schedule a chance to meet in person and interview me. I would use this opportunity to voice my discontent with Children's Hospital. We would meet at my home, on a sunny summer afternoon... What could it possibly hurt?

She's a friendly, quiet, well spoken, and educated woman... A wolf in disguise. She explains how the hospital had made a call to her agency, and that the hospital was concerned about my behavior. She asks me about my relationship with the hospital, and asks my version of the situation. I explain how the hospital's refusal to acknowledge myself and my wife, in our daughters care and treatment, has caused me to want to transfer my daughter to a different hospital. I explain the poor level of treatment, not being informed about our daughter's change in treatment and updates, and the lack of respect for our family. The fact, that they disregarded us as parents, and treated our daughter as an independent child. After all I was banned from visiting my fragile child at a most significant time in her life. She is only 6 weeks old, and has never been with her Mommy and Daddy completely. She needs both her parents to be by her side... This has impacted our family as a whole. My wife's post partum depression has been partly triggered by these events which have kept her from her child. I have become over–whelmed by the chain of events. All the responsibilities of attending my recovering wife, consoling her depression, to maintaining her health, and keeping her blood pressure at bay. Then having to deal with the specifics of my daughter's health and treatment. And to top it off, the level of disrespect and in–consideration from hospital staff in every style, shape, and form. She actually, for the

MOMENT, UNDERSTOOD ME AND BEGAN TO COMPLIMENT ME ON MY COMMITMENT TO MY FAMILY. IT WAS AMIABLE, AND I WAS ASSURED BY HER, THAT SHE IN NO WAY WAS GOING TO TAKE MY DAUGHTER AWAY. AND THAT SHE WAS ONLY DOING HER JOB TO FOLLOW-UP WITH THE CALL THAT WAS MADE TO HER AGENCY. SHE EXPLAINS THAT SHE HAS TO KEEP THE CASE OPEN FOR A ROUTINE 30 DAYS, AND THAT AFTER WHICH SHE WOULD BE CLOSING OUT THE CASE. AND IF I NEEDED ANYTHING I HAD HER PHONE NUMBER. IT WAS A PLEASANT VISIT... SHE SEEMED VERY NICE.

# SIX

At this moment I'm dealing with the weight of the world. I am searching for a possible hospital that would take my daughter into their care, and hopefully it would be closer to home. But my wife is not fully grasping what is going on, with the chain of events that have occurred. My wife was born with an extra chromosome... Which is diagnosed as triple-X chromosome syndrome. What that means is that she has a slight learning disability, and does not fully comprehend things at a normal rate. You wouldn't even notice her disability until you observe the difficulty she has in filling out forms, or reading complex and antagonizing paperwork. She has to be told numerous times a specific subject, before it actually sinks in and she can understand it... sometimes it may only last for a short time, and eventually she forgets the whole subject. It can be rather difficult at times. Especially when explaining serious issues and getting her to be on the same page. But her condition also adds a factor into her self-esteem, and causes her to have insecurities, by way of feeling "stupid"... especially when people are rude to her when she has to ask or be asked a particular question numerous times to understand. So she struggles with this disability, and I myself struggle with it too... Indirectly but most definitely. I try explaining to her how we have to transfer our daughter to a better hospital, but my wife does not agree with this decision. She's been told by the social worker, and the doctors at the hospital, that if we were to transfer the baby to another hospital she may die! She's told that our daughter is a medically fragile baby, and must be treated by professionals. She is told that the only hospital with such credentials is Children's Hospital. This is what my frightened wife is told, and buys into it as if it were on sale... At this point it becomes a power struggle between my wife and I, and she feels she's the mother and has the right to decide for her daughter's safety... Daddy must hit the backstreet, on this one. As hurtful as it is to have your wife choose to listen to a "professional" rather than her husband, I can only accept the blame on her condition for wanting to go against me. The doctor's advice to her to not transfer our daughter, is more based on money and reputation, rather than my daughter's safety... And the truth is that Lucile Packard Hospital in Stanford is another well credited hospital (with possibly greater health care professionals) that can treat our daughter. My daughter in no way was facing death, or had any danger that prevented her from being transferred. Her condition was fragile, but not life threatening at this point. She was greatly improving, and was close to being released from the hospital. But when told by your daughter's doctor the contrary, and not knowing between truth and deceit (due to a slow comprehension) it can easily persuade a person to follow medical advice instead of embracing "possible" death of your newborn child. She love's our baby girl, and doesn't want to risk putting her life in danger... That was the reality she was believing. And no one was going to change her mind about it. And even though the hospital had banned me from seeing our daughter... My wife was still welcome to visit her. And visit her she does.

*Ring Ring*... The social worker from Social Services (or CPS) was calling me to inform me that it was necessary for me to be taught how to operate an oxygen monitor that my daughter would be taking home upon discharge. And also I must complete training for infant CPR, as a precaution. Since I am banned from visiting the hospital, I must obtain the training on my own, and at my own expense. I explain to her my financial situation and the inconvenience of having to pay... I am disabled and only receive a monthly social security check. (My financial status is almost obsolete.) I barely make enough to get by. So she tells me that she will see if her agency can pay for the classes, since I'm not accountable for not being allowed into the hospital to attend the classes. Which I thought was very helpful, and I thanked her for her help. My wife would be receiving the training at the hospital, and would be fully aware of how to operate the oxygen machine, and how to apply CPR incase of an emergency once the baby was discharged. Things seemed to be in place, and working fine. My wife and I were working on our relationship, as I was still upset with her decision to keep the baby at Children's Hospital. The strain of birth and post-partum depression had also taken a toll on our intimacy and communication. We were working together to make things better between us... A slow but worthy cause. We were both very anxious to have our daughter at home, and not have to deal with the hospital staff any longer. We were tired of hospitals. We were informed that our daughter would be coming home the following Friday... Finally! We were very excited, and we started making arrangements right away.

# SEVEN

I ordered a cake (tres leches de banana, strawberry, and limon) and had a special "Welcome home Izabela" written across it. My cousin, who lives about 45 minutes away, was going to help bring our daughter home in her car. She helped us get groceries and necessities for the welcoming party. Everything was set into place, and relatives had been invited to a celebration and welcoming to the family... Our newest member "Izabela". Two proud parents, getting everything ready for mija's big day. Her birthday party. That's when my wife gets a call from the CPS worker... There has been a change of plans, and our daughter will not be getting discharged after all. My heart dropped, and my stomach knotted up. This was awful... my wife began to cry. I couldn't believe it, I didn't understand how, or why this was happening. I was devastated. We we're asked to go to the hospital and speak with the doctors about planning a future discharge. The social worker promised me that she would get me a pass to enter the hospital, so that I could speak with her doctors, and get a chance to take the required trainings for my daughters discharge. I agreed to go to the hospital, under the condition that the CPS social worker would be there with us. Partly because I believed she had my family's best interest at heart, and also because I wanted her to observe how the hospital treats us. And possibly have her serve as a witness for me and my family. (I had been considering suing the hospital at this point.)

Five episodes... Five incidents where my daughter aspirated and failed to breathe. Her condition had apparently grown worse over the course of two days! Or so we were being told... I found it hard to believe. I felt they had other motives to keep our daughter longer. They were making a fortune on hospital bills! My daughter had been in the neo-natal unit 2 months already. She was supposed to have gotten released over a month ago. But even if that were not the case, why were we not informed that our daughter had stopped breathing for a period of up to 20 seconds? Five different times! This is what the doctor describes to us at our meeting, with no emotion or sign of sympathy whatsoever. All this in front of a CPS social worker who looks appalled at the thought of a well established hospital failing to meet the needs of two concerned parents. My eyes meet hers as she slowly comes to realize what I've been explaining to her. I softly say "Do you see?" loud enough for only her to hear... She nods her head. To my amazement she speaks out in our defense and lets the doctor have her piece of mind. In that instant, my voice was acknowledged and heard... But only through the voice of a social worker who works for the county. But never the less, I was finally heard. My wife was in tears at the thought of our daughter stopping from breathing, and the thought of losing her... We hadn't even been notified. My wife was beginning to feel disgusted with the hospital, and wanted our daughter transferred immediately. The tension towards the hospital and the doctor was intense. The doctor was forced to leave the room, and assured the social worker and my wife to have our daughter transferred to another hospital... My wife rushes to my arms and cries in my chest. As I try to assure her everything will be ok. She apologizes for not listening to me, and for not wanting to transfer our daughter sooner. But I quickly tell her not to worry about it. Our daughter is our main concern... I forgive her.

## *Change Of Plans*

We arrive to Lucile Packard Hospital along with our daughter. We are respectfully greeted and attended. The atmosphere was noticeably different compared to Children's Hospital. The staff at Lucile Packard were far more courteous and friendly. We had a much better feeling about our daughter being there, rather than at Children's Hospital. Her new doctor asked us various questions about her health, and answered the major concerns we had. I explained in full detail her previous treatment and health issues she has had. And also included recent problems she had begun having. Her belly button had produced a hernia which I was not aware of, until finally seeing her again for the first time since being banned from Children's Hospital. The doctor explains that it is quite normal for newborns to develop umbilical hernias within the first few weeks after being born. But I explain that she is 9 weeks old, and has developed the hernia in the past week or so. He explains that this must have been caused by vigorous crying, where the abdomen tightens and pushes against the umbilical wall. I am surprised and become upset... Our daughter is very quiet, and sleeps for most of her time. (Which is normal behavior for a newborn.) The only time she cries is when she wants to be fed, or have her diaper changed. And my problem with this, is that she has been in the care of trained and employed nurses. And they have failed to properly attend to her, apparently... They must have ignored her cues, and painful cries. Or she would not have produced a hernia. She must have been left unattended for long periods of time, or just purposely left to cry. A cry so painfully loud and unanswered... I can only pray for forgiveness for not being there. For not being by her side to answer her cry. My wife holds our child in her arms, while I record video of them. I sure hoped this hospital was not like the other. The doctor has reassured us to keep us posted on all updates, and to be included in the treatment plan. He gives us a good vibe, and we feel a little bit more at peace. I just wanted this whole ordeal to be over with, and go home... Together.

# *EIGHT*

*Ring Ring* I called the CPS worker to keep her updated on our daughter's care. I thanked her again for helping us get our daughter transferred to a better hospital. She asks about the discharge planning, and I tell her that it all depends on how her recovery goes, and how she does on the test results. As of now everything was looking good, and we were expecting a period of about 2 to 3 weeks before being released. She had already been taken off of the oxygen mask and improving. I was told by the CPS worker that I must find an in-home nurse for my daughter's after care. I did not know about such requirement, but I told her that I would look into it. I was going to ask my new hospital social worker in regards. Our conversation was short and pleasant, nothing out of the ordinary. I made my way to my class. (A training to become a peer counselor.) I attend group meetings and program trainings on how to deal with mental health clients. My goal is to reach youth who suffer from depression and destructive behavior. I myself suffer from major depression disorder, and I know what it feels like to be stressed and depressed to the point where one becomes self destructive. At this point in my life I am making better choices, and have positively changed my life around... With much help from God and my wife. Who has given me a reason to smile and enjoy life. And now becoming a father to a beautiful child, has given me added purpose and direction for my life. My desire is to be a

POSITIVE EXAMPLE AND ROLE MODEL FOR OTHER YOUTH. AND THIS DESIRE HAS TAKEN ME TO GETTING TRAINED TO BECOME A PEER COUNSELOR.

MY WIFE WAS BEGINNING TO SPEND MORE TIME WITH OUR DAUGHTER AT THE NEW HOSPITAL. SHE TELLS ME ALL ABOUT HER VISITS, AND SHOWS ME NEW PICTURES. THE BABY WILL NO LONGER NEED TO TAKE HOME AN OXYGEN MACHINE, AND IS DOING REALLY WELL. SHE HASN'T HAD ANY NEW EPISODES. THIS WAS GREAT NEWS, AND IT FELT LIKE OUR DAUGHTER WOULD BE COMING HOME SOON. IT'S ALMOST HARD TO BELIEVE. THE CPS WORKER CALLED AGAIN TO INFORM ME THAT I NEEDED TO FIND AN IN-HOME NURSE. SHE HAD FOUND ONE OF HER OWN AND HAD HER IN PLACE, READY TO GO. I DIDN'T LIKE THE IDEA OF A CPS IN-HOME NURSE, AND I POLITELY TOLD HER THAT I APPRECIATED HER HELP BUT THAT I WOULD LIKE TO FIND ONE ON MY OWN. I WAS GOING TO SEE IF I COULD FIND A SPANISH SPEAKING NURSE. SINCE MY WIFE AND I ARE BOTH HISPANIC PARENTS, AND WANT OUR CHILD TO LEARN TO SPEAK SPANISH AS WELL. (THIS IS A CULTURAL THING.) SHE EXPLODES... SHE SNAPS BACK WITH CONTEMPT, "I DID YOUR FAMILY A FAVOR, SO NOW YOU NEED TO DO ME A FAVOR, AND ALLOW MY NURSE TO FOLLOW UP WITH YOUR CHILD." I BEGAN TO FEEL UNCOMFORTABLE, BUT I UNDERSTOOD HER COMPLETELY. I HAD BEEN VERY THANKFUL WITH HER HELP, BUT I HAD A CULTURAL PREFERENCE. AND HER NURSE DID NOT FIT THE DESCRIPTION I WAS LOOKING FOR. I TRIED TO COMPROMISE, AND I TOLD HER THAT IF I DIDN'T FIND A SPANISH SPEAKING NURSE, THAT I WOULD GO WITH HER NURSE. SHE AGREES TO THIS, AND WE FINISH THE CALL ON GOOD TERMS. I WAS STARTING TO GET A BAD FEELING ABOUT THE WAY SHE WAS ACTING. HER TONE HAD LEFT ME WITH A BAD IMPRESSION, AND I DIDN'T APPRECIATE THE HOSTILITY. I WOULD LOOK FOR AN IN-HOME NURSE AS SOON AS POSSIBLE.

I LEFT MY NEW HOSPITAL SOCIAL WORKER VARIOUS MESSAGES REGARDING DISCHARGE PLANS. AS WELL AS, CONCERNS FOR HELP FINDING A SPANISH SPEAKING NURSE TO FOLLOW UP WITH IZABELA. ALL TO NO AVAIL, AND NO RETURNED PHONE CALLS. I RECEIVE A CALL FROM IZABELA'S DOCTOR CONCERNING HER DISCHARGE... SHE WILL BE released the following Monday. The joy quickly fills my body, and I was completely excited. I asked the doctor what time she will be released, and she tells me that I can come pick up our daughter at any time on Monday, the later in the evening the better. (Due to the busy mornings.) I explained to the doctor that I was attending classes for employment, but I would try to be at the hospital by 6-pm. "That's fine. Most parents work jobs, and usually come after work to pick up their children, not a problem." I hung up shortly, and gave my wife a call to give her the good news... She couldn't wait! This anticipation to have our daughter at home had gone on for far too long. It's been the longest expectation from the very beginning, and now the time has finally come for our daughter to come home. Our daughter was going to have her Mommy next to her, and be held an enormous amount of times throughout the day... And night. Her Daddy also wants to smother her with kisses and love. And she deserves it. My poor daughter hasn't had her mother's love near her for most of the fragile moments of her life. She has been deprived of her parents... Who adore her! I can't imagine the pain and confusion she has been going through at such an early age. I can only imagine the psychological effects that it will have on her, and pray she turns out ok. I don't want my daughter to have trust or abandonment issues. This was all going to be over soon, and life was going to get better. I placed my hope in God.

*Ring Ring* I answered a call from CPS. I am told to be at the hospital by noon to go over discharge planning with her and hospital staff. I told her I couldn't make it to the hospital until about 6-pm. Since I had a class finale, that I needed to attend in order to receive a certificate. "If you are not there by noon, I am going to take her into my custody." she tells me... Are you serious? "You can't do that, I already discussed this with her doctor and she told me I could be there in the evening." I responded. For some odd reason she didn't believe me, and begins arguing

WITH ME THAT I MUST DO AS SHE SAYS. I HADN'T SEEN THIS COMING... I THOUGHT SHE WAS OUR FRIEND. BUT OBVIOUSLY SHE WAS NOW THREATENING TO TAKE AWAY MY CHILD. I BECAME IRATE. "YOU DON'T HAVE A REASON TO TAKE MY DAUGHTER, I NEED TO ATTEND MY CLASS SO THAT I CAN GET A JOB AND PROVIDE FOR MY FAMILY." THIS WASN'T ANCIENT HIEROGLYPHICS OR OBSCURE ARITHMETIC... I THINK I'M BEING RATIONAL. "WELL IT LOOKS LIKE YOU'RE GOING TO HAVE TO MISS YOUR CLASS. WHAT'S MORE IMPORTANT, YOUR DAUGHTER OR YOUR CLASS?" SHE HOLLERS BACK. I WASN'T TOO SURE SHE UNDERSTOOD MY RESPONSIBILITY IN SUPPORTING MY FAMILY, OR AT THE VERY LEAST THE IDEA OF COMPROMISE. I DECIDED TO NEGOTIATE WITH HER, "I WILL HAVE MY WIFE BE THERE AT NOON. I WON'T BE THERE UNTIL AFTER MY CLASS. I WILL TRY TO GET THERE RIGHT AWAY. YOU KNOW I DON'T HAVE A CAR." MY FRIEND HAD AGREED TO TAKE ME TO PICK UP MY DAUGHTER AFTER CLASS. (HE ATTENDED THE SAME CLASS.) BUT THIS DID NOT HELP MY SITUATION. SHE AGAIN, VERY RUDELY AND WITHOUT EMPATHY, TOLD ME THAT SHE WOULD TAKE AWAY MY CHILD IF I WASN'T THERE. "I DON'T HAVE TO BE THERE AT NOON, I CAN BE THERE AT ANYTIME ON MONDAY. I ALREADY TALKED TO THE DOCTOR. I HAVE TO PROVIDE FOR MY FAMILY, I'M TRYING TO BETTER MY LIFE. WHAT'S WRONG WITH YOU? ARE YOU IGNORANT?" THIS IS WHERE SHE BECAME VERY EXPLOSIVE... "YOU DON'T KNOW WHO YOU'RE MESSING WITH. I HAVE THE POWER TO TAKE AWAY YOUR DAUGHTER AND PUT HER IN FOSTER CARE. I TOLD YOU THIS IS MY JOB, I DON'T TAKE IT PERSONAL. I REALLY DON'T CARE ABOUT YOUR DAUGHTER, OR YOUR FAMILY. I COULD CARE LESS. YOU EITHER DO WHAT I SAY AND BE THERE, OR YOU CAN DEAL WITH THE COURTS." I REALLY HADN'T SEEN THIS COMING... SHE HAD SEEMED SO FRIENDLY AND CONCERNED. HOW COULD SOMEONE BE SO FALSE, AND HIDE WICKED INTENTIONS. TWO FACED DOESN'T GIVE A DESCRIPTION JUSTICE... MORE LIKE SNAKE FITS BETTER. I GAVE HER MY PIECE OF MIND, AND ASKED HER HOW SHE COULD LIVE WITH HERSELF. TO GO HOME TO HER KIDS AND HUSBAND, WHILE AT WORK SHE'S A DEVIL IN THE FLESH... I ASKED HER HOW SHE WOULD FEEL IF SHE WERE IN MY SHOES, AND WERE FACED BY HAVING HER KIDS TAKEN AWAY. SHE DIDN'T GIVE ME AN ANSWER, BUT HER SILENCE WAS ENOUGH FOR ME. I KNOW ONE DAY IT WILL CATCH UP TO HER. WHAT GOES around comes around. The Bible teaches that "we reap what we sow". And every evil deed we commit in life has to eventually be paid for... And this I trust.

Sunday night, my wife spent the night at the hospital with our daughter. She wanted to be there for her discharge, and didn't want to be late... So she stayed the night. In the morning things were hectic as always. The busy morning schedule, and the fact that it's Monday... A lot of catching up to do from the weekend. My wife was feeling cheerful and excited. She got breakfast, and returned to our daughter's side. The baby's nurse and my wife, had been conversating much over the past weeks, and had become acquainted. They were discussing how exciting it was going to be to have our daughter home finally, when the hospital social worker suddenly showed up. She spoke to my wife rudely, and in a hostile tone (the baby's nurse noticed this as well) "Your husband has been leaving me a lot of messages. It seems he's angry that I haven't returned his calls. I don't like his attitude and I will have security escort him out, if he acts like how he did at Children's Hospital." My wife notices a security guard standing by the door. My wife tells her, "He is only concerned for his daughter. You haven't returned his calls, and I know he has been trying to reach you. I don't know why you have to bring security with you. We haven't done anything." My wife try's to keep herself calm. The worker rudely responds, "I spoke to you about her discharge, and explained everything to you. I don't have to speak to him. You should communicate with him, and tell him what I told you. There's nothing else for me to say to him." Which wasn't true, there was still a lot more to speak about. Such as finding an in-home nurse, help filling out forms concerning medical insurance, and explaining information on future follow up visits. My wife told her this, and explained my concern. "He feels like you're ignoring him. I told him a little bit of what you told me, but I didn't understand all of it. He has his own questions he wants to ask you." Nothing out of the ordinary, just a few basic concerns. A phone call of no longer than 10 minutes would have been enough, but I guess maybe it was not part of her salary. (And she obviously wasn't doing charity.) The worker became frustrated, "I will not tolerate your behavior, and you need to leave the nursery. I will have a talk with CPS about your disrespect. Someone please get security." The hospital worker was obviously flaunting, and expressing her power to have her removed. My wife became upset, and started to look around the room. To her comfort, everyone in the room was feeling the same way as my wife. The nurses were disgusted with how the social worker was acting. So my wife decided to speak out and tell the social worker how she felt. "Do what you have to do. I haven't done anything wrong. I have witnesses." The worker stormed out... In a ball of fire (more or less). The nurses came near my wife and gave her supportive words of encouragement. They were all very sympathetic, and were busy down-talking the social worker. But they quickly changed the subject to focus on what was more important... Our daughter was finally going home.

# NINE

What happened next is indescribable... Only horror. "Your daughter isn't going home with you today. I am placing a hold on your daughter. You are no longer allowed to visit her here at the hospital, and tell your husband as well. You are both banned. If he comes on the premises he will be arrested. You both need to attend a meeting tomorrow to discuss where your daughter will be placed." These words echoed, over and over in my wife's brain until she began to hyperventilate. She began to have what is called an "anxiety attack". Tears erupted, and it became uncontrollably hard for her to breathe. A tiny grin appeared on the face of the CPS worker, who not only a few weeks ago was consoling her fears about our daughter's health conditions. "I'm sorry" she adds with her smirk... The sarcasm only adds to the pain in my wife's chest. My wife leaves the room, bumping into walls, and almost collapses along the way. My poor wife was heart broken. To her surprise a security guard was standing near by, waiting to approach her. The CPS worker came out of the room, and got along side the security guard. It was time for my wife to leave the hospital. She was no longer allowed to be there, or see her daughter... My wife begins to plead with the CPS woman. She begs the worker to at least let her see her daughter. "Why are you doing this? I thought you wanted to help us. Now you say you're going to take away my daughter, and with no emotion. You know how much we've gone through, and how long we've been waiting to take her home with us... Why?" Tears ran down her face and sobs of sadness filled the air. And for a short moment the CPS worker became somewhat human. She allowed my wife to be able to visit the hospital, "But only as long as you tell your husband not to come to the hospital. If he shows up, he will be arrested." The CPS worker insists on banning me from the hospital. And my wife having no choice, agrees to this... She doesn't want to lose her daughter. If even just the chance to see her, and be by her side, she will do whatever it takes.

*Ring Ring* I got the call... My wife was crying uncontrollably. She could barely speak. Every other word was choked by a sob. I finally made sense of what she was saying... I became furious. I couldn't believe what I was hearing. My mind began to race, and I tried to figure out how to deal with it. My daughter has been placed on an emergency hold! They had taken custody of our daughter without a warrant and without any charges. They had taken her without the help of a single police officer. The CPS worker had suggested to her agency to place our daughter in foster care. They had set up a meeting for the following day, to figure out what would happen with her. My only child, my first child, my daughter... I was backed against a wall. I am extremely protective of my loved ones, just as is any father. Although new to being a Dad, I take my role seriously. This is my family who was being threatened. My wife was devastated, and she begged me to do something... I began to feel helpless. I told her not to worry, but who was I kidding? I got on the phone and called some of my family members. I needed their help and support, I couldn't allow for the system to take away my daughter. I made my way to the hospital and parked down the street. I waited for my wife to come out... This was chaos. I couldn't believe the social worker would actually go to these extremes. I didn't see the basis, or how it could even be possible. I was beginning to lose my calm... "Why is this happening Lord?"

# TEN

TEAM DECISION MEETING (TDM)... THAT IS THE FORMAL TERM FOR THIS MEETING WITH CPS. I HAD ARRANGED FOR 3 OF MY COUSINS, MY AUNT, A FAMILY FRIEND, AND MY WIFE TO ATTEND THE MEETING. MY MOTHER WOULD HAVE FLOWN OUT TO ATTEND AS WELL, BUT I DIDN'T WANT TO INCONVENIENCE HER. (SHE LIVES OUT OF STATE.) AND MY WIFE'S PARENTS WERE NOT ON GOOD TERMS WITH US, SINCE THEY HAD NEVER APPROVED OF OUR RELATIONSHIP. DUE TO MY APPEARANCE, MY FINANCES, MY SOCIAL STATUS, AND JUST ABOUT EVERYTHING IN BETWEEN. SO IT WAS NOT A BRIGHT IDEA TO INVITE THEM TO A BASHING PARTY. AS FOR ME, I WOULDN'T BE ATTENDING THE MEETING. I, IN NO WAY, WANTED TO PARTICIPATE ANY LONGER WITH CPS. I HAD REALIZED CPS WAS NOT A GROUP OF PEOPLE YOU COULD TRUST. I DIDN'T WANT ANYTHING TO DO WITH THEM. AND I DIDN'T FEEL SAFE IN THEIR BUILDING. I CHOSE TO SPEND THE DAY SEARCHING THE INTERNET FOR A LAWYER, AND OTHER HELPFUL TIPS ON DEALING WITH CPS. AT THE MEETING, THE SOCIAL WORKER HAD BEEN REPLACED BY A NEW WORKER WHO WOULD BE HANDLING THE CASE FROM NOW ON. (WHICH DIDN'T MAKE MUCH SENSE.) I WAS BEING VERBALLY ATTACKED AND ABUSED BY THE AGENCY. MY FAMILY DID THEIR BEST TO DEFEND ME. THEY TRIED TO EXPLAIN OUR SITUATION, AND HOW HARD IT HAD BEEN HAVING OUR CHILD IN THE HOSPITAL FOR THE PAST 3 MONTHS. MY FAMILY KNOWS HOW MUCH I LOVE MY DAUGHTER, AND ALL THE EFFORT I HAD MADE TO PROVIDE FOR MY WIFE AND DAUGHTER. BUT ALL OF MY FAMILY'S ATTEMPTS TO REMEDY THE SITUATION, LANDS ON DEF EARS. THE AGENCY WANTS TO PLACE MY DAUGHTER IN FOSTER CARE... BUT they wouldn't explain why. They don't give my wife or family a reason why my daughter was being detained. Probably due to the fact, that they didn't have a valid reason. My family offered themselves as a possible placement for Izabela in the meantime, or at least until the court matters were resolved. No one wanted my daughter to be placed in foster care, except of course for CPS. They continued to insult and attack my character, and even took a few stabs at my wife without regards or any remorse. This is standard CPS procedure. It was nothing personal in their eyes... It was just their job. The meeting lasted about an hour and a half. The matter would be left for the courts to decide where Izabela would be placed. My family was willing to submit to background checks and home inspections, to avoid my daughter being placed into a foster home. They left the meeting and arrived at my house after a long, draining afternoon. They explained what had happened... I began to feel horrible, and humiliated. My character had been butchered. My integrity shattered. I was completely embarrassed. The agency had made it seem as if my daughter would not be safe in our home, yet would not give a reason as to why. My family did not seem the same towards me. I could feel their disapproval. I thanked them for their help and their willingness to take my daughter into their home. They would let me know how the CPS interviews went. They had been scheduled interviews ASAP. The hospital would only keep our daughter a few more days, and she needed to have a place to go. Our court wasn't until next week. So it was urgent for my family to get cleared. I didn't want my daughter to be placed into foster care, and I much rather her be with family than a complete stranger. This had all happened with such short notice, and I only had a few days left to find a lawyer... The weight of the world had once again hopped on my shoulders.

# ELEVEN

THE FOURTH OF JULY WAS AWFUL. MY DAUGHTER WAS PLACED INTO FOSTER CARE. IT HAD ONLY BEEN 3 DAYS SINCE THE TDM MEETING, AND MY DAUGHTER WAS BEING TAKEN BY A COMPLETE STRANGER TO AN UNKNOWN LOCATION. "GOD BLESS AMERICA"... THE IRONY. I WAS JUSTIFIABLY LOSING MY CALM, AND MY PATIENCE WITH THE WHOLE SITUATION. THE AGENCY HAD TAKEN ADVANTAGE OF THEIR AUTHORITY AND CONTROL. THEY HAD COMMENCED THE BACKGROUND CHECKS AND INTERVIEWS WITH MY FAMILY, AND MY FAMILY HAD BEEN CLEARED FOR PLACEMENT... BUT THE AGENCY ALLEGED THAT I MIGHT NOT BE THE FATHER OF IZABELA. THEY TOLD ME THAT I SHOULD BRING MY PROOF OR DOCUMENTATION TO COURT, SO THAT THE JUDGE COULD DECIDE IF I WAS THE PRESUMED FATHER OR NOT... UNBELIEVABLE! I HAD THE DECLARATION OF PATERNITY FORM THAT I HAD SIGNED WHEN MY DAUGHTER WAS BORN, AND THE HOSPITALS HAD THIS DOCUMENTATION AS WELL. MY DAUGHTER BORE MY LAST NAME. BUT CYNICALLY THE CPS AGENCY DID NOT HAVE SUCH PAPERWORK. AND THEY WERE NOT INTERESTED IN REVIEWING THE PROOF THAT I HAD... THEY SAID FOR ME TO BRING IT TO COURT. THEY HAD ARRANGED FOR A FOSTER MOTHER, WHO WAS ON HER WAY TO THE HOSPITAL, TO PICK UP MY DAUGHTER. THIS WAS WHAT THEY HAD PLANNED FROM THE START, AND WHAT THEIR PRIME GOAL HAD BEEN. AND NOW THEY WERE JUST GOING ALONG AS PLANNED BY WHAT HAD BEEN DECIDED BY THEIR AGENCY. MY FAMILY BEING INTERVIEWED AND SCREENED HAD ONLY BEEN STANDARD PROCEDURE, AND BASICALLY JUST TO COVER THEIR LEGAL OBLIGATIONS. THEIR INTENTIONS HAD ALWAYS BEEN TO PLACE OUR newborn child in foster care. Where she could be placed for adoption, and the agency could make their quotas. Babies are much easier to get adopted... And my daughter was only 3 months old. Our dreaded fear had now become reality. We pleaded and argued with the agency (over the phone) telling them what they were doing was wrong, but all to no avail... When dealing with CPS, it is a losing battle. Their politics are not moralistic, nor legalistic. Just the fact that they have denied my daughter and my family "kinship care rights", or the no warrant seizure, goes beyond the law... It is unconstitutional. I can't even consider celebrating the Fourth of July. My firework bundle takes a rain check... There will be another occasion. (Just not this one.) We receive a phone number to the foster mother, from the agency, but are urged not to call her more than once a week. My wife, by this time, is under a lot of stress. I can observe her mental stability deteriorating. She has been suffering from a lot of anxiety. This was not an easy situation for anyone to endure, and much less for a first time mom. Showing symptoms of post partum depression, and recovering from giving birth, she was now dealing with losing her beloved child... I don't wish this heartache on anyone. Our family didn't deserve this treatment... No one does. I tried to do my best to console her. But I was beginning to lose her trust. I hadn't been able to achieve getting our daughter back and remedy the situation. And things had only begun to get worse. She pushes me away... It pains me. I couldn't bear to see her so hurt. I wished I could do something to bring her joy back, anything to bring her happiness... My only option, as of now, was to get a lawyer. I spent the rest of the day searching online.

I came across a few lawyers in the area, some were Hispanic. I gave those lawyers a call first. I finally got in touch with one, and explained my situation... He seemed professional, and familiar with handling CPS cases. So we set up an appointment to meet and discuss the case. Since I didn't have much time to be searching (court was in 3 days), we agreed to meet over the weekend. And I was to bring cash and sign forms, in order for him to take our case. He was being considerate, given the circumstances, to meet over the weekend. (He didn't usually work on the weekends) I emptied my savings, and called my brother... I needed to borrow some money. I swallowed my pride, and explained to him the situation I was in. After much venting, he was very sympathetic and understanding. He was willing to help. He was saddened by the whole situation and shared my pain. He was going to wire me some money... I thanked him dearly. He asked me to keep him updated. He offered to help us in any way, and hoped everything turns out ok. (I am very thankful with God for giving me the family he has given me.) Although this lawyer was expensive, my daughter is worth more... And I would give everything I own to keep her. I put my trust in God, and tried to remain positive. Our daughter belongs with my wife and I... Our God given right.

# TWELVE

THE LINE WRAPS AROUND THE SUPERIOR COURT BUILDING. IT SEEMS POLICE HAVE BEEN ACTIVELY HANDING OUT TICKETS, AND ARRESTING CITIZENS. THE LINE TO GET INTO COURT WAS RIDICULOUS. IT WAS A LITTLE BEFORE 9–AM, AND EVERYONE IN LINE WAS ANNOYED WITH THE WAIT. THIS IS THE HASSLE EVERYONE WHO RECEIVES A TICKET OR FACES CHARGES, HAS TO GO THROUGH... IT'S ANTAGONIZING. WAITING IN LINE TO GO THROUGH A MEDAL DETECTOR COULDN'T BE ANY LESS CONVENIENT. WE HADN'T SLEPT MUCH THE PAST FEW NIGHTS. IT HAD BEEN EXTREMELY TENSE AND STRESSFUL. WE FINALLY GOT INSIDE, AND BEGAN TO WAIT AGAIN. WE SAT IN THE LOBBY NEAR THE COURTROOM. MY LAWYER SOON ARRIVED AND APPROACHED US. HE EXPLAINED TO US HOW THIS PART OF THE COURT PROCESS IS CARRIED OUT, AND THEN GOES INSIDE THE COURTROOM TO FIND OUT WHO THE AGENCY HAS BEEN APPOINTED AS A COUNTY COUNSEL. HE ALSO NEEDED TO REVIEW THE PETITION THAT THE AGENCY HAD FILED AGAINST US. HE BROUGHT US EACH A COPY, AND TOLD US THAT MY WIFE WOULD BE GETTING APPOINTED A PUBLIC DEFENDER. AND SINCE I HAD ALREADY HIRED A LAWYER MYSELF, I WOULDN'T NEED A PUBLIC DEFENDER. HAVING TWO LAWYERS WAS GOING TO GREATLY HELP US, AND BE AN ADVANTAGE TO BOTH LAWYERS, HE TOLD US. SINCE, THEY WOULDN'T HAVE TO CARRY THE BURDEN OF THE ENTIRE CASE ALL ON THEIR OWN. THEY WOULD BE ABLE TO ASSIST EACH OTHER, AND WORK TOGETHER. THIS SHOULD BENEFIT OUR FAMILY AND THE CASE, AND MY WIFE AND I AGREED TO KEEP THE PUBLIC DEFENDER THAT MY WIFE WILL BE APPOINTED. WE BEGAN TO READ THE CPS REPORT, AND QUICKLY WE WERE APPALLED... IT WAS VERY disturbing. The report consisted of me being violent in nature... CPS had been told by the Children's Hospital social worker that I was violent, and belligerent towards staff there. To the point where I had to be banned! The facts were sickly twisted. They stated that they felt our home was not a safe environment for a medically fragile child. They seemed to be suggesting possible domestic violence. They had concluded this from a "supposed" argument at the hospital, between my wife and I. They also included, that we as parents, didn't know how to take care of a child. Since I, as the father, had not taken any of the teachings on how to feed our daughter (she needed a thickener to be added to her formula) and also hadn't received any trainings on precautions or safety measures. My wife was described as "spacing out" during her teachings, and was accused of not knowing how to properly care for a medically fragile child. The CPS worker had also mentioned in her report, the fact that my wife's parents did not approve of me. This revealed that her parents had also spoken negatively about me to both the CPS worker, and the hospital social worker. The report was entirely based from Children's Hospital's perspective, and the added fact that I had been banned. They even included that I had been banned from the new hospital, Lucile Packard. (Which was after the CPS worker had placed the emergency hold on my daughter.) They were using these circumstances to mislead, and manipulate the judge's opinion of me, to persuade his decision in their favor. This was their approach and sabotage towards our family. I basically was being described as hostile, violent, and abusive. My wife was being described as a spaced out, naive, and abused wife. Due to this dynamic, my daughter being placed in our care, would put her life at risk... Completely unbelievable! No child abuse, no sex abuse, no child neglect, no domestic violence, and no arrests... Yet my daughter has been placed on an emergency protection hold, and consequently placed in foster care. The entire report had been alleged a month prior, and reported to CPS from Children's hospital. Why

HADN'T THEY PLACED HER ON HOLD THEN, WHEN THEY FIRST RESPONDED TO THE ACCUSATION, INSTEAD OF WAITING AN ENTIRE MONTH? (IF IT WAS THAT SERIOUS AND CONCRETE.) I SURE HOPED THE JUDGE WOULD SEE THROUGH THESE FALSE ACCUSATIONS, AND MAKE A FAIR AND LAWFUL RULING. I BEGAN TO PRAY TO GOD, AND ASKED HIM TO HELP OUR FAMILY THROUGH THIS WHOLE PAINFUL ORDEAL. MY FAITH AND TRUST WERE WEARING VERY THIN... BUT I WAS LEFT WITH FEW OPTIONS. I ONLY WANTED WHAT WAS MINE... MY DAUGHTER. "LORD PLEASE BRING MY FAMILY JUSTICE."

THE NEW CPS WORKER, WHO HAD BARELY BEEN ASSIGNED OUR CASE, WAS PRESENT IN COURT. IT WAS MY FIRST ENCOUNTER WITH HER, AND I WAS NOT EAGER TO BECOME HER FRIEND. WE HAD BEEN INTRODUCED, AND TALKED SHORTLY IN THE HALLWAY BEFORE COURT HAD STARTED. SHE DID NOT COME OFF AS A FRIENDLY PERSON. THE JOB OF THE EMERGENCY RESPONSE WORKER, WHO WAS THE PREVIOUS WORKER, WAS TO TRY TO BECOME TRUSTED, AND GAIN AS MUCH INFORMATION AGAINST A FAMILY AS POSSIBLE. THAT WAS WHY SHE HAD DONE SUCH A GOOD JOB AT BEING FRIENDLY, AND SEEMED GENUINELY HELPFUL. BUT NOW THAT HER PART WAS DONE AND OVER, THE TRUE MASK OF CPS WAS UNVEILED IN COURT. THIS NEW WORKER WASN'T HIDING HER CONTEMPT TOWARDS US, AND DISPLAYED AN AIR OF SUPERIORITY. QUITE ARROGANTLY AND CRUDE IN HER DEMEANOR. MY LAWYER ADVISED THAT THIS RUDE BEHAVIOR FROM THE WORKER WAS A TACTIC THAT CPS USES TO MAKE PARENTS REACT NEGATIVELY, AND USE IT AGAINST THEM. THEIR GOAL IS TO PUSH PARENTS TO THEIR BREAK, AND THEN POINT IT OUT TO THE COURTS AS A SIGN OF NEGATIVE BEHAVIOR ISSUES. STANDARD, BASIC CPS STUFF. NEW TO ME, BUT ROUTINE CPS REGIMEN. THEY WEREN'T FOOLING ME ANYMORE THOUGH. I COULD READ BETWEEN THEIR LINES NOW. I KEPT MY DISTANCE, AND LET MY LAWYER DO ALL THE TALKING. WHEN THE CPS WORKER TOOK THE STAND, I WAS EAGER TO FIND OUT WHAT SHE HAD TO SAY. SHE HAS HAD THE CASE FOR ONLY A WEEK, AND IT WAS NO SURPRISE THAT HER WHOLE TESTIMONY WOULD BE HEAR SAY. BUT I WAS SURPRISED THAT IT WAS EVEN ALLOWED IN COURT. MANY OF THE QUESTIONS SHE WAS ASKED, SHE wasn't even able to answer. Due to insufficient information on the case... Which, wasn't fair to the severity of the case. It wasn't fair to our family, and wasn't fair to my daughter. Izabela's life was at stake here. Being detained in foster care, and with the possibility of being adopted (depending on the outcome), her life was in the hands of a corrupt CPS agency. At 3 months of age, my daughter had no clue of what was going on, or what was being planned for her... Or, more accurately of how she was being robbed. Robbed from her parents, and robbed of her rights.

We stepped out of the courtroom after the worker's spiteful charade, and conversed with our lawyers in the hallway. Court had been adjourned until the next day. The lawyers were both shocked with the social worker's testimony, and puzzled at the same time by the whole case. They didn't feel that what the agency was doing was right. And they didn't feel CPS had a strong enough case to keep Izabela from us. They tried to give us encouraging words and hope, but they also told us that these cases can take months... And sometimes years. Their main goal was to get Izabela home safe with us. We needed to keep our attitudes positive, and try not to let the agency get under our skin. "Be patient, and try not to give them the reaction they are wanting to get from you. Just smile and keep things respectful." My lawyer tries to give us some advice, and keep us from getting upset towards the agency. (Easier said than done.) But we kept it in mind, and made our way home. Tomorrow would be another day. Hopefully the case would get thrown out, and we could finally have our daughter home. Our baby needs to be at home with her Mama and Papa. Her room had been decorated specially for her. Purple painted, wooden letters of her name, stretch across the wall in her room above her crib. Embroidered with butterflies and ribbons. Her crib has a pink, animal print comforter with the side skirts, and a window valance to match. On top of her dresser, we placed a matching animal lamp (It was

PART OF A SET) AND PHOTOS OF HER IN PICTURE FRAMES. WE HAD THE BABY CAMERA MONITOR SET UP FACING THE INSIDE OF HER CRIB, READY TO MONITOR HER WHILE SHE SLEEPS. EVERYTHING WAS IN PLACE, AND READY TO GO... NOW WE JUST NEEDED IZABELA. I SPENT THE REST OF THE DAY PRAYING WITH DIFFERENT FAMILY MEMBERS AND PASTORS OVER THE PHONE. I WAS TRUSTING GOD WOULD ANSWER OUR PRAYERS, AND FULFILL HIS PROMISES IN HIS WORD. THIS WAS JUST PART OF "TRIAL AND TRIBULATION". A TEST TO BUILD MY FAITH, AND MY TRUST IN HIM. I COULDN'T LET THIS ATTACK DEFEAT MY FAITH OR DESTROY MY FAMILY. I WOULDN'T ACCEPT THAT INTO MY LIFE. ONLY GOD COULD MAKE THIS WHOLE SITUATION RIGHT. AND I THANKED HIM FOR IT... BECAUSE I KNEW THAT HE WOULD.

# THIRTEEN

"THEY WANT TO MAKE A PROPOSAL. THEY ARE WILLING TO ALLOW IZABELA TO LIVE WITH YOUR WIFE, AS LONG AS YOU ARE NOT LIVING IN THE HOME." MY LAWYER BEGAN. HE GENTLY TRIED TO SWAY MY DECISION, AND BRING AN UNFAIR RESOLUTION TO THIS WHOLE AFFAIR. NOT TO MENTION UNJUST, AND UNLAWFUL. I DIDN'T AGREE WITH THIS DEAL, AND NEITHER DID MY WIFE. WE'RE A FAMILY, WHY SHOULD I BE EXCLUDED FROM MY OWN FAMILY? I HADN'T DONE ANYTHING WRONG. "THEY WANT YOU TO FINISH THE REQUIRED TRAININGS TO PROPERLY TAKE CARE OF IZABELA, BEFORE THEY ALLOW YOU TO RETURN TO THE HOME." HE ADDS. I DISAGREED WITH THIS... WHY COULDN'T I TAKE THE TRAINING, AND LIVE WITH MY DAUGHTER AT THE SAME TIME? I WAS CONFUSED. MY WIFE HAD TAKEN THE TRAININGS, AND THE ONLY SPECIAL REQUIREMENT TO TAKE CARE OF OUR DAUGHTER, WAS THAT HER FEEDINGS REQUIRE A THICKENING GEL TO BE ADDED TO HER FORMULA. (IT COULDN'T POSSIBLY BE THAT DIFFICULT.) THE BABY COULD BE WITH THE BOTH OF US, AND MY WIFE WAS AWARE OF HOW TO PREPARE HER BOTTLE. SHE COULD EASILY TEACH ME HOW TO MAKE HER BOTTLE... IT WASN'T ROCKET SCIENCE. AND I WOULD BE WILLING TO TAKE WHAT EVER CLASSES TO END THIS FIASCO. "WOULD YOU BE WILLING TO ACCEPT THEIR OFFER, AND ALLOW YOUR DAUGHTER TO BE WITH YOUR WIFE UNTIL YOU TAKE AN INFANT CPR CLASS?" HE CONTINUED TO ATTEMPT TO REACH AN AGREEMENT. I WAS LEFT WITH NO CHOICE BASICALLY. I GUESS I WOULD HAVE TO ALLOW IT. I WASN'T IN A GOOD POSITION TO BE CHOOSY. MY ONLY CONCERN WAS WHERE I WOULD LIVE IN THE MEANWHILE. "THE AGENCY WANTS THE BABY AND YOUR WIFE TO reside with her parents (my wife's parents). Since if your daughter lives in your home, it would be a lot easier for you to visit her there. And it would be harder for the agency to make sure that you aren't living in the home." I was dumbstruck... This was a lot to take in. I'm not on good terms with her parents. We have a love/hate relationship, without the love... And it's extremely mutual. Her father was an abusive man during my wife's childhood that has caused severe mental trauma on my wife. He is a very stern and strict man... A bit of a control freak. With all the put downs, and the manipulation, he has scarred my wife on an emotional level. The root of her insecurity comes from a bad childhood. And her father stood in the main spot light... Front and center. He was the type of father that never showed affection. Never gave his daughter any compliments, or that he loved her... Quite the opposite. Partly, her insecurities were formed by his constant insults. He had called her "stupid" for most of her life. Her mother was always scolding, and upset with my wife as well. Demanding her to do dishes, cook, and clean. Threatening her that her father would be upset with her if she didn't do it quickly. Harsh words and reproach, was what greeted her everyday in her home. This had been her life since early on. Not being good enough, and living in her academically achieving brother's shadow, wasn't easy. It was not her fault she was born with a disability... But her parents didn't realize that. Maybe because they weren't fully aware of her condition, and didn't have the patience to deal with it. Or maybe they were just disappointed... But this was a distant reality. It had been about a year and a half ago, that my wife and I had moved in together. I took her away from that negative environment, and showed her love. I tried to motivate her, and helped her feel confident within herself. She had lived a very sheltered and deprived life. She wasn't very happy, and her actions and demeanor showed it. But this began to change when I came into her life. She was only 24 years old, and finally discovering life in a brighter light.

Maybe this was her parent's true contempt, or her mother's jealousy. Either way, they never liked me. Now I was being asked to allow my daughter to stay in their home, along with my wife... I was uncomfortable with this idea. Her parents don't have a good report card, if you know what I mean. I was faced with a tough decision. I decided to just fight it in court, and see if the judge would see things our way. Hopefully get a fair decision. "Alright. It's your case. I think you should just take the offer they're giving you, but I'm going to do what you ask. I'll do what I can... Get ready to be on the stand." He wasn't very pleased with my choice to fight the agency in court. And it wasn't comforting. He was supposed to be on my side.

# FOURTEEN

I guess this was it, my turn to voice my side of the story. I could feel their eyes of contempt on me. This was my chance to tell the truth. I had been taking a beating by my opposition. Piles of paperwork, notes, and misguided reports from the agency. My wife gave her testimony before me, and it went very well. She was obviously nervous at first, but after a while she became very fluent with her responses. I thought she gave a clear description of the whole scenario, and shed truth to the stack of lies the agency was precluding. I was pleased with her performance. "You did good Babe." I told her, before my turn to go up on the stand. She asked me if I was sure... She didn't think she did so well. She complained that she was too nervous. (Women are very nit-picky.) I assured her that she did great. I proceeded to take my place on the stand, and placed my hand on the Bible. I made my oath to give the truth. "The whole truth, and nothing but the truth"... "I do." My lawyer begins an array of questions, and orchestrates facts to give a better, more accurate picture. He enters exhibits as evidence. Pictures, letters, medical records, and a training certificate. My testimony was then cross examined by the county counsel. (Grill would be more accurate.) She asked about my relationship with Children's Hospital. She probes my brain for hostility. She accuses me of harassing the hospital staff there, and putting my hands on a nurse attending my child... At the time of the incident with the nurse in question, I was the one complaining about that particular nurse. She had grabbed my daughter's head aggressively with force, in front of my wife and I. The moment she did it, I grabbed her hand, and told her to stop! I asked her repeatedly not to grab my daughter's head like that, but the nurse didn't stop. She didn't care how we felt. She turned a simple procedure into using aggressive force. I asked to speak with the doctor immediately. He arrived by my daughter's bed side shortly after. We were very concerned for my daughter's safety, and had many questions for the doctor about her health. She had suffered from an episode of aspiration, when the nurse was helping my daughter adjust her head position. But she had done it very forcefully. The nurse stood there quietly. She seemed very nervous, trying to smile apologetically. I decided not to report her to the doctor, for what she had just done. My wife and I requested for that nurse not to be re-assigned to my daughter. We asked this in front of the nurse, to the baby's doctor. And that had been the end of it... Apparently now it was being twisted to meet the agency's portrayal of me, and put me in a negative light. I started regretting not reporting the nurse. (For documentation purposes.) The county counsel's next jab was to accuse me of ripping a breathing tube out of my daughter's nose that could have caused my daughter to aspirate. Corrupting the truth, and making it fit to their persona of me again. The reality was that my daughter had a piece of tape placed underneath her eye, that was so close to her eyelid, that it caused for her eye to not open completely. We had noticed her discomfort. (As her parents, we pay close attention to detail concerning our daughter.) I had asked to speak with her attending nurse, and asked the nurse to fix the tape that was attached to her feeding tube (not a breathing tube). "There's nothing wrong with the tape. She's fine. I did it myself." The nurse replied arrogantly, and then walked away. I called out to her, "Can you get the charge nurse? I don't want you watching our daughter anymore." She heard me, as do other nurses and parents in the nursery, but she decides to ignore me. And I hear the words, "Get her yourself." underneath her breath. (Typical staff behavior from Children's Hospital.) I decided to just do it myself. My wife and I wiped my daughter's cheek with a wet rag, and I gently pulled the tape back. Making sure that the tube stayed in place. After we were successful, I asked a nearby nurse where to find more tape. My daughter's attending nurse overheard, and rushed to where our daughter was. She practically pushed my wife out of the way, and began to accuse us of making her having to do her job all over again. I asked her to leave my daughter alone. I didn't like how she was handling her. She was being too rough with her, and rushing through her job. I wanted her to get the charge nurse. "I'M NOT GETTING THE CHARGE NURSE. GET HER YOURSELF. DON'T TELL ME HOW TO DO MY JOB." I ended the conversation, and went to look for the charge nurse. My wife and I expressed our concern to a supervisor, and asked to have that particular nurse excluded from attending our child. This was what had happened, and thankfully I had proof. I had a picture that showed the tape near her eye, affecting her vision, moments before I detached it. The county counsel then began to turn the focus on my marriage. She asked if I had ever called my wife "stupid", or if I had ever done any other name calling. I admitted that I had. I didn't deny it. I had called her names in the past during arguments. Nothing uncommon, we're human. That's what happens in marriage, people argue. That's as far as it gets, and that's as far as it goes. I love my wife. If anything, I have been her best friend. I always apologized to her after an argument, and she did the same as well. I guess, in child protection services, relationships must be perfect... Which is unrealistic. An over embellished expectation of reality. Just because our relationship wasn't perfect, who gave them the right to invade our personal space? This experience was intrusive, and disgraceful. After several questions I was finally done being interrogated... The judge had a few final questions. He asked me what I felt was the cause that led my family into court. "Lies" I respond... He wasn't too happy with my answer. He decided to ask me about my tattoos. He confronted me about my choice of tattoos, and persuaded me to accept his opinions. He suggested, how my daughter might feel to see her father inked... Or how other parents might feel about me. He described how my appearance might affect her. And also how it had already affected how others viewed me, and treated me. Which was true. People are generally intimidated by me. They view me as a gang member, criminal, drug dealer, and a killer... "Armed and dangerous". Which isn't true, but looks and first impressions go a long way. Stereotypes, and the stigma that movies and TV create, play a big role in how people think. Being a Latino in California isn't an added bonus. People's perception of me, causes them to have a defensive attitude towards me. The judge makes this point clear, and hopes that I've learned something from all of this. "Yea I have. I'm trying to help youth who are getting into trouble, and help give them other options to cope with what's affecting them. And now I'm thinking about also working with foster kids who have been taken from their families. Since now I can relate with them on how it feels to be separated from your family, and dealing with CPS" I reply. I can tell he's surprised by my answer. He looks offended. He thanks me, and asks me to step down and take my seat.

# FIFTEEN

The judge has reached his decision. He has heard the testimonies, and reviewed the evidence. The attorneys have all made their closing arguments. It is his understanding that Izabela is a medically fragile child that requires special feedings. As well as many follow up appointments. Due to all her medical conditions and needs, he felt it was his responsibility to ensure that Izabela would be safe. He felt it was not in my daughter's best interest to be separated from her mother, and was putting Izabela back in my wife's care. Under the condition that my wife not leave her side at all. Izabela would be under my wife's constant care and responsibility. She would not be able to leave her with anybody else, for any reason whatsoever. If she failed to do so, Izabela would be removed from her care, and lose custody to the state. As for me, I was found to be the "presumed father", and was not allowed to visit with Izabela until I received infant CPR training. My wife and child would have to reside at my wife's parent's house until I completed the training. After which time, the agency would have discretion to remove the restriction, and allow Izabela and my wife to move back into our home. I also was not allowed to visit with my wife and daughter, until the matter was resolved in court. If I wanted to visit with my daughter, I would have to set up a supervised visit with the agency. But I would be allowed to attend Izabela's medical appointments, or any appointments concerning my daughter. The judge was not going to make Izabela a dependant of the court. This was the judge's ruling. (The very exact deal I had been offered by the agency.) We would have a follow up court date in 2 weeks to review if I had completed the training, and any further reports. Court was adjourned. My wife was extremely happy... I on the other hand felt mistreated, and abused. I felt left out. I was being kept from my daughter, and restricted from my wife. This wasn't fair. I didn't plan to set up any supervised visits. Just the thought of it made me uncomfortable. I would just have to appreciate the visits during my daughter's medical appointments. I was pretty upset about the whole outcome. My wife tried to cheer me up, "Everything's gonna be ok. We're gonna all be together soon. She's gonna be with me in the meantime. It's better than having her in foster care with some stranger. Don't worry mi amor." She gave me a smile. It made me feel a little better, and I knew that at least my daughter was going to be with her Mommy... And we were getting a step closer to having the baby at home. I planned on getting my infant CPR training completed ASAP.

Our lawyers were discussing with CPS on how to set up for my wife to pick up our daughter. While my wife and I waited patiently in the hallway. After they came to an agreed place and time, my lawyer came over to speak with us. He congratulated us on getting our daughter back. He explained to my wife that she must meet with the CPS worker, back at her office, to go over plans to pick up Izabela. He was shocked that the judge had ordered our daughter into my wife's care. "This usually doesn't happen. Families usually take months before their child is placed back into their home. You guys are very lucky." he says. I asked him if he thought we could get the case dismissed. But he didn't think that it was very likely. "My guess is that it could take around six months to a year. These things take time. I would recommend that you ask for a public defender, if you don't think you can afford to pay for my services. You know that I charge by the hour. With the court dates coming up, and more to follow, it can get expensive." I began to worry. If the case didn't get resolved quickly, I wouldn't be able to afford it. But I was hoping, and trusting in the Lord that the case will be dismissed. Surely we couldn't lose our daughter when we hadn't done anything wrong. Plus, things were already going pretty good. We had gotten our daughter back, even though the agency was recommending the court to place her in foster care. And the only thing that the judge was concerned about, was us properly dealing with my daughter's health conditions. I asked my lawyer about where I could go to take the infant CPR training. He says, "I will talk with the worker about getting you the locations. Also, you won't have to pay for the training. The agency is responsible for that. It was their recommendation to the judge in the first place. And I'm going to ask her about when you would be able to visit with Izabela." I told him that I had decided not to visit Izabela at the agency's building. I'd rather just see her at her appointments for now. It's only until I can get my CPR certificate, and have her at home anyways. My lawyer tried to urge me to set up a supervised visit, but I refused. He explained that the agency wanted to see how I interact with my daughter, so that they could see that I'm able to take care of her. But from the videos I've seen on YouTube, about CPS workers nit-picking every little thing parents do, and basically hawking every little move they make, I'd rather just visit my daughter in a more pleasant atmosphere. "It would just be too much negativity, and add to my stress. I don't want to visit my daughter like that." I tell him. He understood, although he didn't agree with me nor recommend it. He left me for a moment, and later returned with the worker. She began to ask me some questions, and reproachfully asked me if my wife or I smoked cigarettes... Which we don't. "Are you sure? That's funny. My supervisor said she saw you guys smoking a cigarette outside, before court." She was now accusing us of smoking cigarettes. I hadn't smoked a cigarette in over a year. I had open heart surgery the year before, and was not allowed to smoke during the healing process. I had quit completely. My wife also had to quit smoking during her pregnancy. She had just finished having our daughter 3 months ago, and hadn't returned to her old occasional habit. So I didn't understand where this accusation was coming from. We hadn't met her supervisor, so I wasn't sure how she even knew what we looked like. She was obviously trying to find another reason why our home would not be safe for a medically fragile child. It was another one of their good old tactics... Fabrication. She dropped the subject, and told me that she would look into the classes for CPR. I asked her if I could find a class on my own. (I didn't want to waste any time waiting on her.) She told me that was fine, as long as it was a state recognized training. (Such as Red Cross.) And if I found one on my own, to let her know how much it was going to cost. So that she could put a request into her funds department to pay for the class. She tells me, "I will do my best to do this as soon as possible. As soon as I get back into my office, I will begin working on your case. If you pay for the class yourself save your receipt, and we will reimburse you." We shook hands, and went our separate ways.

# SIXTEEN

So my wife and her parents drove to the agreed location to pick up our daughter. When the foster mother arrived with Izabela, the caretaker didn't look very happy. She was a large woman with dreadlocks in her hair, and multiple piercings in her ears and face. She handed over the baby to my wife along with her things (diapers, wipes, bottles, formula, and medicines). After a few exchange of words, the foster mother drove off. My wife was happy and relieved. She kissed Izabela and placed her in her car seat. My wife rode in the backseat along with our daughter. The ride home was full of joy and loving words. Izabela didn't seem as happy as my wife though. She was looking everywhere, feeling confused. She had spent 3 months in the hospital with nurses, then 5 days with a complete stranger for the first time out in the world, and now she was finally was with her mother. This was new to her, and she was not familiar with it yet. My wife felt a slight pang of sadness. Her daughter wasn't embracing the moment very well... At least not as excited as my wife felt. It was going to take some time for Izabela to open up to her, and form a mother/daughter bond. It was a bit discouraging. When they got home, my wife gave me a call. "Hey babe. I got the baby, she's doing good. I'm feeding her right now." She explained the exchange, and how the foster mother was brusque with her. She hadn't seemed like someone that would be motherly, much less a person that would be recommended by the state's agency. Also she had seen in the diaper bag, all of Izabela's medicines unused. Which meant that the foster mother hadn't given her any. She was supposed to have that medicine applied to every feeding. Without it, she could choke on the formula and aspirate. Izabela suffers from larygomalacia and reflux, which means she has difficulty drinking thin liquids and holding them down. The medicine serves as a thickener to help keep her formula from going into her lungs, and also to keep it from coming back up once in her stomach (known as reflux). So it seems unethical to accuse us as not being suitable to properly take care of our child, remove her from us, and then place her with a complete stranger that doesn't properly give the baby her medicine. Also It's upsetting to me, that I must require CPR training and medical teachings to properly administer medicine to my daughter, before I can have her in my home. Yet this woman that they chose to take care of my daughter, has not done any of the teachings, and isn't CPR certified. She has no medical background whatsoever. How is it possible for the conditions set for me, are not required by anyone else? Although my wife watched a video to learn CPR in case of an emergency, she is not certified. I am being court ordered to learn safety precautions in order to have my daughter. The hospital did not require these trainings, and were only as a safety precaution. For example, I am not certified to apply an oxygen mask in case of an emergency during a flight, yet I am allowed to ride on an airplane. The safety precautions at the beginning of a flight are not mandatory. Much less court ordered. It's insane. Haven't they ever heard of 911? It's called an emergency. If my daughter stops breathing I would rush her to the ER or call 911. I don't need to be certified to do that, its common sense. This was all an abuse of authority, in a system that has too much power. Once again, it's unconstitutional. Nevertheless, I must endure the abuse, and push forward for my daughter and my family.

Red Cross offers CPR trainings. I signed up for the next class (which happens to be the next day) and paid the full amount to reserve my entry. The cost was $60 for a 4 hour class. After I had signed up, I called the CPS worker to let her know. She told me that I was very quick, and that she hasn't started working on my case yet. Because she said that she had been very busy. She said that she would put a request in to her funds department right away, so that I could be reimbursed. "It usually takes about a week or two. So just give me some time to work on that. As soon as you have your certification let me know, so I can put it in my report." I told her ok and we hung up. Our conversation was quick and to the point. I called my wife to let her know that I had found the class. She was glad that I was taking care of it. She was giving the baby a bath, and had spent most of the night getting up every few hours to make a bottle. She had sent me some emails with pictures and video of the baby... "She's so cute. I'm so glad she's finally home. You're gonna love it. I tell her you love her, and I show her pictures I have of you in my phone." She tells me. I became desperate to see her. My heart wanted to have my daughter and my wife home, and have this nightmare be over. The house felt so empty and lonesome without my wife. This intrusion into my family had begun affecting my mental health. I had begun to feel moods of depression and anxiety. I hadn't been sleeping much, and my appetite was close to none. I was very irritable, and dealing with built up anger against the system... I felt violated and victimized. Growing up as a minority in the US is hard. Being taken advantage of by the system is even worse. Especially when it involves your child... I needed to get myself more involved with church. God always heals my pain. When nothing else, or no one else can. Life has been difficult for me, and I have learned to go to God when times get hard. When there are no answers and it seems there's no way out, He gives me the strength to keep trying. The peace I need to stay sane. That's something alcohol or prescription medicine never could accomplish... You can't substitute God. And it took me several years to discover that (and many bottles).

After many attempts on a plastic dummy, I had accomplished properly applying CPR on an infant. And after a short exam on what I had just learned, I became certified. I walked out of that class with a certification card and feeling ecstatic! I quickly called my lawyer to inform him that I had finished the CPR training. I wanted to find out how to get the restriction removed, so that my family could come home. He would call the CPS worker and discuss it with her. She had the power to use discretion and remove the restriction for my daughter to live with me. It would all be up to the worker. So that left me with much room for doubt... Although I had done what the judge had ordered, it would still have to go through the agency's workers and supervisor's approval... It wasn't very promising. After about 15 minutes, my lawyer called me back. "I talked to the CPS worker, and she is going to be giving you a call. She wants to verify that you completed the CPR training. Did they give you some sort of proof?" I told him about the certification card that they gave me. My lawyer wanted me to fax him a copy, and told me to wait for the worker's call. This was on Thursday. It seemed she had forgotten to call me or maybe she got too busy? I didn't know. Either way she hadn't called. Friday came and I decided to give her a call, and see about my wife and daughter coming home. I got her voicemail and it explained that she would not be in her office that Friday... Well that was just great. I wished she had called me the day before, but now I would have to wait until Monday. I was hurt, upset, and sad... All the emotions that were going through me were giving me pain in my stomach. It was going to be a long weekend. By Monday I had been waiting patiently throughout the morning until I finally decided to call. No luck, I got her voicemail once again. I left her another voicemail, and asked her to give me a call as soon as possible. Tuesday I got her call. "I've been very busy the passed few days. What did you want to speak to me about?" She tells me, as though she were annoyed by all my voicemails. I was confused, I was sure she knew about the certification. My lawyer had spoken to her last week and told her about it. "I did what the court asked for me to do. I have my certification. I want to get the restriction removed, so that my daughter can come home." She didn't think that would be a good idea. She wanted me to bring proof of the certification to the next court date. She and her agency had a few new requirements they would present to the court before they allowed Izabela to come home. I pleaded with her briefly, but I didn't want to exhaust myself. I knew that it would be impossible to reason with her or her agency. The fact remained and she would not use the courts discretion to remove the restriction. I would have to wait until the following week, to fight it in court... Lord have mercy. I couldn't win for losing with these people. Their priorities and requirements were illogical, and served no purpose for the greater good of any child. That was the impression they gave me. My daughter had not been harmed, hurt, or abused in any way. What was the need to restrict her from my home? What were the agency's criteria and prime goals for my daughter? Why were they so exigent with her? This couldn't be a valid precaution with their drastic measures, there must be ulterior motives. Such as a paid bonus, quotas, or on a more extensive note: RACISM. Our case didn't meet any criteria or principles from the CPS guidelines to remove a child. So what was the extreme degree and necessity to remove my child? I believe they were crossing a thin line, which is called "Color of Law". How far were they trying to go with all this?

# SEVENTEEN

Two Weeks had passed since the last court date. I had followed through with my requirements to complete CPR training for infants. I was comfortable with my accomplishment, and was ready to be granted my rightful place as Izabela's father. My wife met me in the hallway with Izabela before court started. We embraced, and I quickly reached into the stroller to hold my daughter. My wife's parents were present. They were seated further down the hallway. They openly gave me looks of disgust. (It was common behavior coming from them.) My daughter was dressed up and looking beautiful. It felt good to have both my girls next to me. People would stop to see the baby, and asked for her name and age. "She's beautiful" was everyone's response. "Thank You." Two proud parents, we were blessed to have her... I held them closer. My lawyer arrived, and as routine he entered the courtroom to retrieve the agency's petition. When he returned, he handed me a new report. It was now being focused extensively on my mental health, and the concern that there "may be" domestic violence. Apparently my wife's mother had suggested to the worker that she felt there may be domestic violence. She had also suggested to the Children's Hospital social worker prior to this, that our home was not safe. My wife's mother had insisted for the hospital not to release our daughter to us. This had initiated the concerns for CPS intervention, and lead to the hospital calling CPS. My wife's mother had also been the one who mentioned to the hospital and CPS, the fact that my wife has a learning disability. My mental health diagnosis were also included in the report, as well as past hospitalizations for depression. My past convictions were also added. I couldn't believe they were aiming so low. My prior convictions were more than a year old, the last being a misdemeanor. None of my charges were against my wife or child. I didn't have any charges of domestic violence, assault, battery, sex charges, or crimes against a child. I was not on probation, and had never been on parole. Yet they were trying to use my prior convictions to keep my daughter from my custody... And I thought getting a job was hard. My felonies were being used to disqualify me as a father of my own child. What kind of mentality is that? I think something is terribly wrong with this system and the child protection agency. Child Protection Services has too much power and authority. To be allowed to choose who can be a parent and who can not... They might as well have given me a vasectomy when I pleaded "no contest" to grand larceny back in 2001 (seven years ago) if the conviction was going to determine my legal ability to become a father. I had no idea that it would even become a factor. I couldn't believe my wife's parents had been behind all of this. I didn't think they would do something so evil. Even though they hated me, how could anyone cause for their own grandchild to be taken from their children? My lawyer told me not to worry. He would show the judge my CPR certification that he had ordered me to complete, and do his best to get Izabela and my wife home with me.

"I am going to order a psychological evaluation, and a domestic violence assessment for both parents before I make my decision. I will keep the restriction for the father to remain out of the home. The mother is not to leave Izabela's side, nor have any contact with the father unless at medical appointments. And I will see you all here next month." The judge had adjourned the court, and left me in the same place I had been in since this trial began... Without my daughter. My defense, my progress, and my rights were not being acknowledged. Every request of the agency was being heard and fulfilled. While I was being treated second class. This was looking helpless, and extremely hopeless... I was disappointed in the justice system. Not that I was ever satisfied in the legal system, but this judge was making a mockery of the law. But this was just the realities of the family court system, it was completely biased and favored towards the county and district attorneys. Anyone that has been in my shoes, can swear the truth of it. Dealing with CPS is frustrating and stressful. I stepped out the court room upset, and the first thing I saw was my wife's parents. They were waiting eagerly for the outcome. They seemed to have about as much anticipation as we did, but not for the same results as my wife and I. The CPS worker stepped out of the courtroom and approached them. "Why is the worker talking to your parents?" I asked my wife. She was surprised, and got upset. We could only imagine all the bad things they were saying about me and my wife. "I thought it was illegal for CPS to discuss our case with anyone else?" I asked my lawyer. He told me that he didn't know what the worker and my wife's parents might be discussing, "But yes. That's not allowed by law." He changed the subject and talked to me about the psychological and domestic violence assessment. The CPS agency was going to pay for a psychological evaluation and he wanted me to agree to take the evaluation. He couldn't be serious. I was paying him $200 an hour for bad legal advice and poor representation? "I'm not going to do an evaluation. Why would I help make the case for CPS? Getting an evaluation isn't going to help my case. It would only help CPS if their psychologist writes a negative report about me. I'm not gonna set myself up for failure. And what is a domestic violence assessment?" He couldn't give me a valid answer. Seems he had never heard of one either. He didn't agree with my refusal to cooperate with CPS. He thought my refusal to submit to an evaluation would hurt my case. "MY CASE. Exactly, it's my case. I'm paying you to represent ME. Not the other way around. I'm not going to do any evaluations. They need to work with the evidence they have. Not try to make new evidence." He was offended by my tone. I had not meant to be offensive, but he wasn't listening to me. He was urging me to do something that could possibly affect me. I knew how psychologists worked. I had been involved in mental health care services for a few years. And especially when they have a partnership with the CPS agency, it would only hurt my chances not make them better. I didn't see any strategy in giving in to the agency's request, other than being cooperative... But at what price? He changed the subject, and told me to look into parenting classes. He said it would look good in court and would help the case. "Most these cases end up having to take parenting classes. If you take the initiative to look for classes on your own it would show the court that you are actively trying to take good care of your daughter." This was his best advice yet. I decided I would look into it. We shook hands and agreed to stay in touch. "Don't forget, I will send you the bill for the hours so far. I will see you next month." Right... What a waste of money. I was broke, and I still didn't have my daughter at home. My wife was sad. She had been looking forward to going home... My beautiful wife. We shared the pain of separation, and I tried to console her. I tell her, "I know its hard babe. We just have to wait. Pray to God, only He can help us. Go to church. Be good ok? I love you." We kissed and said goodbye. We would talk later that night.

# EIGHTEEN

My nights were beginning to become lonely. I felt confined. I was forced to sleep alone, once again. Pictures of my daughter on my nightstand, and my wife and I together, didn't suffice. I was deprived of their love... They were my world. My whole life I had looked forward to having a family of my own. Having a wife and children... This was not how I had pictured it. I had given my life to Jesus Christ in December of 2007. My life had drastically changed. I used to hangout and party. Have drinks with my friends, and go out clubbing. I had given all that up. I was now living a Christian life. A married life. Trying to do good, and give back to society. Pursuing a career to be a counselor, and help change lives. This was not part of the plan. I had to drop out of my training to become a peer counselor, because the court trial was taking all of my energy and my focus. It would be almost impossible to sit in a classroom learning how to help others, when at the moment I felt helpless and couldn't help myself. Plus my anger towards the county's Social Services wasn't mixing well with my view of the county. (The training was run by the county's mental health organization.) I began to look into parenting classes. I found a website that was offering parenting counseling. I called the number listed and scheduled an appointment right away. The organization was in the town I lived in, and accepted Medi-Cal. The program even offered in-home visits. I wouldn't have to take the bus to attend the sessions. It was perfect. The counselor spoke Spanish as well, and would be doing an intake interview at my home in a few days. I felt good about this, and thanked God for this blessing. I called my wife to let her know the good news. She was happy about it, but she didn't really understand what it meant. I explained it to her until she understood what the purpose of the parenting counseling would accomplish. They offered help with parenting advice, but also dealt with the stressors of parenting and offered counseling. As well as help addressing any issues or strain that parenting has put on the relationship between the parents. "So I would be able to go to those meetings also? I wouldn't feel comfortable talking about our problems to some stranger. Is he cool? What if he tells CPS about our problems?" My wife had a lot of doubt about the whole idea. She didn't feel safe talking to anyone now that we had been abused so badly by social workers and CPS. She felt if she told the counselor that she was feeling post partum depression and anxiety, the agency would use it against us. I tried to re-assure her that it would be ok. And if she didn't want to talk to the counselor about things she wasn't comfortable with was fine. But the truth was that we needed an outside person to help counsel us. She hadn't been the same since the pregnancy. Our relationship was unbearably strained, and now the separation by CPS was not making things better. Things felt barreling downward, and maybe this counselor could help us. I was trying to hang on to what we had and our future as a family. "It's all gonna work out. You need to talk about the things you've gone through. Like how your dad's neglect and abuse affected you. This counselor can help you. I'm gonna be there for you, but you have to do your part. How can you get better, if you don't deal with what's affecting you?" She heard what I was saying, but she was not fully in agreement. But she would try.

Getting to my daughter's appointments took me longer than my wife. Her parent's would give my wife and daughter a ride to the doctor's office or let my wife use their car. While as for me, I had no choice but to ride the bus alone. I didn't let that prevent me from getting to spend time with my daughter and see my wife. I pleasantly looked forward to attending the medical appointments. I noticed how Izabela was growing attached to my wife, and my daughter didn't like anyone else holding her. She would cry profusely when I attempted to pry her from her mother's loving arms. It was heartbreaking... I began to feel left out. I tried to swallow my hurt, and just keep trying to be there for the both of them. We were following up with her MRI scans, and the doctor was concerned with a black impression on her ovary. She had gotten the scan observed by other specialists in the hospital, and they had suggested that it may be a tumor. They would need more time to do more studies to be completely sure. But either way, the doctor felt that Izabela would need surgery to remove one of her ovaries... We were shocked. My wife started to tear up. Our daughter caught a shiver from the change in atmosphere. I began to gently rub her head, and whispered near her ear to try to calm her. While my wife, began to ask numerous questions to the doctor about the surgery. The doctor guaranteed a successful extraction, and assured us that our daughter would have a good chance of having kids of her own one day. She would go under anesthesia for a few hours, and receive doses of pain medicine suitable for infants afterward. But they would need our approval to go through with the procedure. My wife and I agreed to follow the doctor's medical advice, and gave the approval. She would be scheduled for surgery as soon as they had all the paperwork figured out. Which doing so, would take no more than 2 weeks. The doctor would also take advantage of the time Izabela would be under anesthesia, and fix the protruding umbilical hernia. Killing two birds at the same time... We were left with the devastation. Our poor little girl would be once again hospitalized for about 2 or 3 days. She had already gone through so much at such a young age. Being hooked up to numerous monitors, wires, and tubes. Not to mention all the tests and medicines. This time she would be getting surgery... It was a lot to bear. We would be allowed to stay near her bedside overnight. Which was comforting... My wife didn't want to leave her little "Mama's" side. And at least we would all be together.

The surgery was a success. It lasted close to 4 hours. We waited in the lobby while mija went under the knife. We met up with her soon after, and stood by her side. My wife was saddened to see her with all the wires and bandages. I was in disbelief. I couldn't imagine how my daughter must have felt. I felt terrible for her. She had gone through so much, and she was only 4 months old. (Technically she would be two months, being that she's premature.) I was just glad that the surgery went good, and that our daughter had come out OK. Izabela was heavily sedated and was knocked out. Her nurse was being very gentle with her, and was kind enough with us as well. We would be at the hospital overnight, and find out the next day when she would be released. It all depended on her progress. One of the nurses gave us a tour of the hospital. The hospital had designated parent sleep areas, a computer area, books and magazines, and of course the cafeteria. The staff were all very friendly and considerate. Very different to the hospitality we had been treated with at Children's Hospital... And the least to say about the hospital where my wife gave birth. This was much more pleasant. My wife and I took the opportunity to spend time together. We ate lunch then took a walk to the mall close by. It was a beautiful summer day, and for the moment my problems had gone away... Or at least I was not dwelling on them.

My wife and I slept through the night... Together. A comfort I had been missing since the judge's unfair restriction. We slept next to my daughter's hospital bed. The hospital provided a pull out bed next to her bedside. It was very pleasing. I got to wake up next to my family. My daughter was still asleep. Her medicine had kept her sedated for most of the past day. I had made sure to give little "Mama" her pain medicine on time. I had also gotten the hang of making her bottle. It had only taken me two tries to get it figured out, and be able to do it myself. Her doctor eventually made her rounds and came around to our daughter's bedside. She gave us good news. Her progress had been going very well and she would be ready to go home later that evening. They just needed to fill out some of her paperwork and prescriptions... My wife was glad, but she wasn't too happy. It seemed she wasn't ready to leave. We had enjoyed spending our time together, and being a family. The staff and nurses had all been very nice and helpful. My wife gave me her sad face... It was going to be very hard to say goodbye. But for now we had no choice. The state threatened to take away our child. And so we would have to do things right, and follow the rules in order to beat the case. We took various pictures, and made the best out of our remaining time together. Before we left, I took the opportunity to ask Izabela's doctor and nurse for a written letter about our hospital stay. I thought it would help if I brought some documentation to court. I kissed my baby goodbye and told her I loved her. I hugged my wife and she hugged me back hard. She didn't want to let me go. "I'm gonna see you soon babe. Love you Ok?" I told her. She pouts back, "OK. Love you too." Then we kissed and parted ways... The ride home was very heart wrenching. I had already begun to miss them. I didn't want to go back home to find another lonely night. This needed to end soon. My soul was taking a beating, to a fight I didn't even initiate. And no matter what I did, it didn't seem to work in my defense or remedy the situation. I just had to keep my trust in God... Jesus Christ.

# NINETEEN

Court was nearing, and I had been acquiring evidence for my case. I had obtained the medical records and evaluations from my hospitalization from earlier in the year. The psychological evaluation done at the mental health hospital should serve as the evaluation the judge was requesting. The progress notes written by the staff there should help my case tremendously. The notes written about me were very positive. They spoke of my good behavior and being helpful to other mental health clients. They described me as pleasant and respectful to staff. This was going to go completely against the persona the CPS agency was portraying of me. I was happy and felt hopeful with my new piece of evidence. I had also gotten a reference letter from the director of a youth organization I had been actively involved in. I was highly esteemed and labeled an asset to the organization, for my contribution and involvement. My evidence was beginning to paint a better and more accurate picture of my character. I had taken my lawyer's advice, and had gotten enrolled in a parenting counseling program. The counselor had paid me a visit at my home. We discussed the requirements for the program. (Such as income and health insurance.) I was eligible for the program, since I was a first time parent to a newborn. My mental health history made me a candidate for the program. The interview with the counselor went very well, and he was very understanding about my situation. He gave me some sound advice and was eager to help me out. He would be meeting us once a week. And we would be meeting at my home once the baby came home. In the meantime our family would have to meet at his office. I would run it by my lawyer and make sure that the CPS agency would allow it. That was going to be the hard part. They didn't want me to have any contact with my daughter whatsoever. The fact that I could visit my daughter at medical appointments was the judge's ruling, and was contrary to CPS suggestions. Which, this was the only privilege that the judge granted on my behalf. But I tried not to let it get to me. My faith in God was helping me think positive... God is my judge.

The day of court had finally arrived. My wife and I met in front of court, and we stood in the dreadful line waiting to get in. My daughter was getting more beautiful everyday. Her hair was starting to grow out and her eyes were like a chameleon. They would change with the climate or with what she was wearing. They ranged from blue, to green, to hazel. We had never seen that before. My wife had also pointed out that the baby had 2 cowlicks. I was shocked. I had never seen that before either. We giggled a bit at the back of the baby's head. It was kind of funny. An Asian woman had pointed it out to my wife, and told her that in her country it meant that the baby was special. I guess it also meant that the baby would be headstrong in some definitions. In Latin country's it means that she has a bad temper. I just thought it was funny... I didn't believe all the hype. My wife gave me a good shove and told me not to laugh. I was feeling good, looking forward to ending this trial. The agency hadn't proved their case in any way, shape, or form. They were merely speculating and assuming. Based on my mental health and prior criminal convictions... And of course my skin (the tattoos) and ethnicity. This was factual. I had been reviewing numerous reports from both CPS and the hospitals, and I had come across the notes taken from the CPS worker. She had written

THE WORD "WETBACK" ON HER NOTES ABOUT ME, TAKEN FROM THE TEAM DECISION MEETING WITH MY FAMILY. I DIDN'T THINK IT COULD BE ANY CLEARER THAT THERE WAS SOME RACISM INVOLVED. I SHOWED MY LAWYER WHAT I HAD FOUND, AND HE WAS DUMBFOUNDED. I ASKED HIM TO POINT IT OUT IN TRIAL. I WANTED TO BRING IT INTO EVIDENCE. "WHAT IS THAT GOING TO PROVE? HOW IS THAT GOING TO HELP YOUR CASE? SHE MUST HAVE WROTE THAT FROM WHAT SOMEONE SAID AT THE TDM." IS WHAT HE TOLD ME. AT THAT POINT I BEGAN TO QUESTION HIS SINCERITY IN REPRESENTING ME, AND QUESTIONED HIS HERITAGE. (HE WAS ALSO A LATINO.) I RESPONDED "MY FAMILY WOULD NOT REFER TO ME AS A WETBACK. THEY DON'T USE THAT WORD. IT'S OFFENSIVE. WHY WOULD THEY CALL ME A WETBACK? THE WORKER IS OBVIOUSLY A RACIST. THAT'S A MOTIVE TO BE UNFAIR, AND IT'S ILLEGAL." HE SAID HE WOULD PRESENT IT IN COURT, BUT HE DIDN'T FEEL IT WOULD BE ADMISSIBLE. OR THAT IT WOULD BENEFIT THE CASE. I DIDN'T REALLY HAVE MUCH CONCERN FOR HIS OPINIONS OR ADVICE ANYMORE. I GAVE HIM THE EVIDENCE I HAD ACQUIRED. (SINCE HE SAID HE DIDN'T HAVE TIME TO DO IT HIMSELF.) HE LOOKED OVER IT AND TOLD ME HE WOULD DO WHAT HE COULD. HE TOLD ME TO HOPE FOR THINGS TO GO GOOD. MY WIFE WAS DISCUSSING WITH HER LAWYER. SHE HAD BEEN DEALING WITH MUCH ABUSE AT HOME FROM HER PARENTS... ANYTHING RANGING FROM INSULTS TO THREATS. MY WIFE REPORTED EVERYTHING TO HER LAWYER. THE LAWYER KNEW THE TOUGH LIVING SITUATION AT MY WIFE'S PARENTS. HER PARENTS WERE CONSTANTLY MONITORING HER AND THREATENING TO TELL THE CPS ABOUT HER BEHAVIOR. HER MOTHER WOULD TELL MY WIFE SHE WASN'T A GOOD MOTHER TO IZABELA. SHE WOULD POINT OUT EVERY LITTLE THING SHE DID WRONG, OR THAT WAS DIFFERENT FROM HER OWN TECHNIQUE. MY WIFE WOULD SPEND HER DAYS CRYING, AND FEELING OVERWHELMED. HER PARENTS WOULD NOT LET HER LEAVE THE HOUSE, OR THEY WOULD CALL THE CPS WORKERS TO INFORM THEM. NOT THAT SHE WASN'T ALLOWED TO LEAVE THE HOUSE, BUT THAT WAS HER PARENT'S RULES, AND NOT THE COURT'S. THEY PRACTICALLY SPOKE TO THE SOCIAL SERVICES WORKER ON A DAILY BASIS TO REPORT ANY NEGATIVE BEHAVIOR FROM MY WIFE, AND SUPERVISED HER ABILITIES AS A MOTHER FOR THE AGENCY. HER PARENTS AND THE AGENCY WERE ON the same team. They both wanted us to lose custody. My wife's mother was obsessed with keeping the baby for herself. Her father was obsessed with making my life miserable. He seized any and every opportunity. If it wasn't enough dealing with CPS, having her parents as the devil's helpers only made things worse. They were standing at the very end of the hallway speaking to the CPS worker privately. I was amazed at the hatred. My only peace of mind was my faith in God. I was not going to let them rob me of my peace. The Lord is my deliverer, my savior, and my refuge. I wasn't going to let two instigators change my belief.

We stepped into court and took our seats. The process, had called for the CPS worker to take the stand. She was under direct question by each attorney. They each took turns examining her testimony. She had given some answers that were beneficial to my defense. She had stated that me and my wife were positive and appropriate in caring for our daughter. This was taken from her report from doctors and nurses that performed the surgery a few weeks prior. And although she now had this evidence, she still maintained her recommendation to keep me out of the home. "For me what's missing is his mental health status. I need to know if he's getting treatment, why he was hospitalized earlier this year, and any information on prior hospitalizations. That's my main concern." She was all out of reasons. It no longer was about me being able to properly care for my child, but now it was all about my mental health. The reports had indicated that both parents were cooperating with medical staff, going to all appointments, and maintaining the well-being and health of Izabela. She had gotten a copy of my most recent hospitalization. The reports indicated that I was interned for depression, and I had not been prescribed any psychiatric medication during my stay nor upon my release. She also had the treatment plan and report from the counselor that would be dealing with our family's parenting and counseling. Her recommendation stood firm. "I don't know whether the counselor is addressing domestic violence concerns. Or if the father has completed a domestic violence or mental health assessment" She insisted. Even though she had never witnessed, or had any evidence of any violent behavior toward my wife, child, or anyone else. She maintained a need for domestic violence treatment. My lawyer went ahead and submitted the page where her notes indicated the term "wetback". She was questioned about it, and affirmed it was her handwriting. But her next response slid her under the radar, "That is from a conversation, I'm not sure with who I had with, but it was statements that the father had made to someone else." I was amazed. She was suggesting that I had made those comments to someone else about myself. Which she could not remember who... Unbelievable! I hadn't even been at the TDM meeting. The judge was not even interested in the least bit as she was being questioned about it. He was fumbling around on his desk as she answered questions. For a moment I thought he might have been texting.

After much questioning the CPS worker was excused. My lawyer and my wife's lawyer both motioned for a dismissal. My lawyer rose and spoke upon my behalf, "I don't think the agency has shown a need for the minor to be made a dependant of the court. There has been no showing of a likelihood of extreme hardship to this minor, or substantial risk that this child would suffer serious physical harm or illness. I am asking that you dismiss the case." To which the judge DENIED. "I find that there is substantial evidence, actually, and that the minor is at risk. This is a difficult and unusual case. We have two parents that are clearly extraordinarily devoted to their daughter. And yet I can't help but worry about what would happen if this court were not to take jurisdiction. And while there is no evidence of physical battering and both parents have testified to that, we have no evidence to suggest otherwise. That is why there is a need for a domestic violence assessment. There are some indicators that are present in the relationship, such as put downs, and controlling factors. And for these reasons I am going to take jurisdiction. I am going to continue the placement of the baby with the mother under the condition that she not reside in the same home as the father. The social worker can remove that restriction once the father has completed a psychological evaluation and both parents are addressing the issue of domestic violence. Once those things are in place, my concerns will no longer be there." And just like that my world was taken from me.

I was devastated. I could not believe what had just happened... I was speechless. My lawyer was busy speaking to me about filing for an appeal, while I was too busy stuck in a daze. Or better yet a knockout. He kept trying to tell me that I could still get my daughter back if I did everything that the agency told me to do. "Hey we tried our best. You did what you could. You have a six month review coming up, so you need to start doing everything they ask you to do so that you can look good when we come to court. Try to set up supervised visits so that they can see that you're a good father." He went on and on... I don't think he understood what had just taken place in there. My rights had been completely violated, my family was being torn apart, and he had failed as an attorney. And to top it off he says to me, "Well you know that so far you have only paid me for the first 10 hours. We agreed that you would pay me in monthly installments, since I know your financial situation and I'm trying to be helpful to your needs. I will calculate the hours we have spent in court, and the hours I have spent reviewing for the case. And I will send you the bill. You don't have to pay me all at once, just pay me what you can. We'll work something out. I know you're going through a lot right now, so we'll just discuss this later." I'm sure he would. I was not interested in money at that moment. I had bigger things to deal with. My family was being destroyed. My hope and my faith was crushed! I didn't know what to do anymore. I had been praying and trusting in the Lord, and now this... It was a huge blow. My wife hugged me. "It's gonna be ok. All this is going to be done soon. We just have to keep trusting in God. Look on the bright side, at least now you can see your daughter and be with her." She says to me. I became upset with her. "Didn't you hear what just happened in their? We lost! It's over. I'm done with this. I'm not gonna do what CPS tells me. I haven't done anything. They can't just take our daughter away. I don't care what that stupid judge says." She began to cry. She didn't want me to give up. She says to me, "Even though we can't live together, the judge didn't say that you can't visit us. Now we can spend more time together. At least it's something right? Please don't give up on our family. Your daughter needs you. And I know that she loves you." My wife was right. The judge hadn't ordered any stay away or restriction from visiting with my daughter. I had lost all my composure in court, that I had lost focus. The only thing I could hear at that moment when the judge was giving his ruling was the fact that he was taking jurisdiction over Izabela. Now that my wife was telling me something positive, my spirit lifted a little... But I was still feeling the intoxication of despair. My wife's lawyer had come over to us and apologized for our loss. She wanted to let us know that I was able to visit with my daughter now. And also, that my wife was able to move where ever she liked. She didn't have to stay at her parents. The lawyer knew that the situation at my wife's parents had become hostile and overwhelming. "It would be a good idea for you to start looking for a place to live. You don't want your parents to make more difficulties in the case. You want to look your best when we come back for our 3 month review." She told my wife. I would have to find a place for them to live. I wouldn't be able to visit them at her parents, and I wouldn't want them to find out that I'm seeing my wife and daughter. Her parents would be the first persons to report it to CPS. And as of now, it wasn't a restriction in the ruling, nor did I want CPS to make it a request. We would have to be discreet in our encounters, to attract the least amount of attention from CPS. This was going to be like sneaking into a G-rated movie. It was unethical and quite absurd. What is this country coming to? There are so many laws and law officials, and yet no one to truly govern. Can't anyone see the flaws in this family court system? I can only pray for God to help me and my family... "Lord give me strength to take it one day at a time."

# TWENTY

The entire day I spent contemplating, and debating on whether to help my wife rent a bedroom from strangers or possibly relatives, or to move out of my own home and become homeless. Since, it was their home too, and I was the one being cast out. I struggled with the thought of being homeless again. I had been homeless for many years in my early adult life. And I had come so far. I had acquired section 8 about a year ago, and had been keeping a good report with landlords and neighbors. I no longer was homeless. The stability a home offers is essential for a healthy life and happiness. "Home is where the heart is." And I was busy building mine. My daughter was my first pillar. CPS was robbing me of my dreams and ambitions. I had been working on my homeowner program certification through section 8, and I only needed to attend 2 classes until I would become eligible to purchase a home. I would be a homeowner at the age of 26. I was trying to set a solid foundation for my growing family, and providing for our future. But this would have to come to a screeching halt, and take a drastic detour. I was going to have to remove myself from the lease and lose my section 8 voucher, in order for my wife and child to have a place to live. This was their home... Our home. I was being excluded, and removed from my family. I would have to go down to the housing authority the next day, and begin doing the paperwork. I spent the rest of the day thinking of where I would go live once I moved out.

This was extremely disturbing. The thought of being homeless was what landed me in the hospital earlier that year. I had become overwhelmed and depressed because I was homeless. I was on section 8 at that time, but no one wanted to accept section 8 vouchers. And the ones that did, were not happy with my criminal background and credit check. It was very difficult. It took a toll on my monthly paycheck filling out many applications and paying the credit check fees. Plus I was staying out of hotels, and it was becoming expensive. By the time I ran out of all my money, I still had no leads on a place to live. I interned myself into a psychiatric hospital for help. I had felt hopeless, and carried the burden of not being able to provide a home for my family. The hospital understood my situation, and the overwhelming stress of it. Caseworkers began to work on getting me housed. There had been no need for medications, since my problems were related with stress and not anything psychological. The case workers were very helpful. I had made friends with staff, and was even offered a job working with them. I would need to attend a training in order to become certified. That was when I got involved in training to become a peer counselor. As soon as I was released from the hospital I signed up for a well known and accredited program run by the county. I was accepted few months after and had been looking forward to accomplishing the goal I had set for myself, in order to get a job and provide for my family. But of course, now plans had changed. And I was going to be homeless again, and my best hope for finding a room to stay in would be at my cousin's 4 bedroom home. Which her house was almost 2 hours away from where I lived... But I began to make calls and get things in order. My wife and daughter would have a place to come home to. That was the most important thing. I placed their needs before mine. I would just have to find a way to survive.

Weeks had gone by. I had moved out by the 1st of the month. That was

WHEN THE CHANGES ON THE LEASE TOOK AFFECT. I WAS NO LONGER ON THE LEASE AND HAD GIVEN UP MY SECTION 8 VOUCHER TO MY WIFE. THAT MEANT IF THINGS DIDN'T WORK OUT WITH COURT, THE CHANGES WOULD BE IRREVERSIBLE. AND OF COURSE IF MY WIFE AND I WERE TO EVER SPLIT, SHE WOULD KEEP THE VOUCHER. IT WAS NOT A SLIGHT DECISION. THERE WERE TREMENDOUS REPERCUSSIONS, AND IT WAS A VERY SERIOUS DECISION. BUT I WAS WELL AWARE, AND HAD MADE MY MIND. IT WAS IN THE BEST INTEREST OF MY WIFE AND DAUGHTER TO HAVE THEIR OWN PLACE. AWAY FROM THE CONSTANT MONITOR AND REPROACH FROM MY "IN-LAWS". MY SECTION 8 CASE WORKER COULDN'T BELIEVE WHAT I WAS DOING, AND ASKED REPEATEDLY IF I WAS SURE. HE KNEW THE DIFFICULTY I HAD GONE THROUGH TO GET HOUSED, AND THE PRIOR HOSPITALIZATION. HE WAS QUESTIONING MY RATIONALITY. "I'M JUST MAKING SURE. I DON'T WANT YOUR MENTAL HEALTH TO SUFFER, AND YOU WIND UP BACK IN THE HOSPITAL. IT'S GREAT WHAT YOU'RE DOING FOR YOUR FAMILY, BUT YOU HAVE TO ALSO CONSIDER YOUR OWN HEALTH." HE POLITELY OFFERED HIS SINCERE ADVICE. IT WAS WELL HEARD, BUT I ASSURED HIM THAT I WOULD BE OK. I'M NOT A STRANGER TO STRUGGLE OR HARD TIMES. I WOULD HAVE TO ENDURE THESE HARD TIMES FOR MY FAMILY'S SAKE. I WAS NO LONGER A SINGLE MAN, WHO ONLY HAS HIS OWN RESPONSIBILITIES. I CARRY THE BURDEN OF TWO EXTRA LIVES. THAT'S PART OF BEING THE HEAD OF A FAMILY. THEY DEPEND ON ME. AND I WANTED WHAT'S BEST FOR THEM. EVEN, IF IT WAS AT MY EXPENSE.

MY NEW HOME HAD GRANTED ME A NICE PLUSH SOFA BED. IT WAS NOT AS COMFORTABLE AS MY QUEEN SIZED ORTHOPEDIC BED BACK HOME, BUT IT WOULD HAVE TO SUFFICE. I WAS IN NO POSITION TO BE CHOOSEY. I WAS THANKFUL TO HAVE THE OPPORTUNITY TO LIVE WITH MY COUSIN AND HER FAMILY. HER DAUGHTERS WOULD ASK TO SEE THE BABY CONSTANTLY. THEY WERE ECSTATIC ABOUT MEETING THE BABY. HER THREE DAUGHTERS WERE AGES 3 TO 1 YEARS OLD (EACH A YEAR APART). IT WAS A CONSTANT PLAYGROUND IN THE LIVING ROOM... CONVENIENTLY WHERE I HAD TO SLEEP. THE EARLY MORNING YELLING AND SCREAMING, AND LOUD TV DIDN'T BOTHER ME MUCH THOUGH. IT WAS A LOT BETTER THAN BEING YELLED at by a large security guard at 6–am. It was miniscule in comparison. My wife would come and visit every so often. She would take the Greyhound, and stay for a few nights. We would attend church in town, (that some of my relatives are actively involved in) and we would just hang out with family. The kids would gather around the baby and show her their toys. Everyone stopped to admire the baby. It was as if she had that special gift, to stop a crowd dead in its tracks to catch a glimpse of her beauty and smile. Our little "Mama" was always so happy, and smiling. She was a friendly baby. But that was just as long as you didn't try to hold her. She only allowed her mother to carry her. (She was spoiled and picky. Just like her Mommy.) My wife and I talked about the case together. She had been given a psychological evaluation, and was set for counseling treatments. "My doctor is annoying. She just sits there and stares at me. It's as if she's trying to peer into my brain. It's uncomfortable. I just sit there and just look at the clock. And she asks some weird questions. It's just so uncomfortable going there." She doesn't like it one bit. The agency had referred my wife specifically to that doctor. And it's not hard to understand why. It was just the same dirty tactics they used to frustrate parents, in order to fabricate professional evidence. I myself had started a counseling treatment in town. I had done so without the help of the CPS agency. My Medi–care was covering the expenses. So far the sessions had gone well. I was primarily discussing the impact CPS had taken on my mental health. As well, as the damage CPS has done to my family. He seemed to feel that it was pretty much self explanatory. He would be willing to write a letter for me so that I could bring it to my next court date. Since this had been one of my requirements, to be actively engaging in treatment. The other was a psychological assessment, which I decided to request from the parenting counseling services we had attended for 4 weeks. This was my most recent assessment I had completed. It would have to be enough, and serve as a psychological assessment, because that's what it really boiled down to anyway. We had to drop the parenting program once we lost the case, because I became homeless and had to move to another county. It would be too difficult finding transportation every week to attend the meetings. But the counselor was still eager to help my family beat the CPS accusations, and reunite our family. He had made me copies of his intake assessment, and after I read it I was sure it would suffice. A 3 month review was to take place in another few months, almost a week or two after Thanksgiving. I decided to just wait for court to present my new evidence that I had acquired, in order to allow me to live with my daughter. I knew that trying to deal with the new CPS worker was not going to grant me that. They had assigned us a new worker once the trial had ended. It was part of the agency's process. But CPS workers are all the same, I didn't trust them either way. I would just have to wait for court to present my progress to the judge. My wife began telling me many rumors about the new CPS worker, who had been assigned to us to do family maintenance and reunification services. She was an older woman who was practically despised by everyone, even including her own co-workers. Attorney's also hated to deal with her. It was no surprise that we got stuck with the worst of the worst. By this time they had obviously received my "notice of claim" to sue them. I had mailed out 6 or 7 copies certified mail, to each worker, supervisor, and director handling our case. So I was sure this new worker was in some sort, a way to spite us for the claim to sue the agency. In fact they had received my "notice of claim" a week prior to the judge's unfair and biased ruling. I wouldn't be surprised if there was some corruption lying behind closed doors. His ruling was highly suspicious. Even judges are subject to breaking laws. They may fool the public and even myself, but they can't fool the Lord Almighty. For He is all knowing, and everyone must pay for their wicked deeds. The truth always comes to light. You can't hide from God.

# TWENTY ONE

My wife and I had each been assigned a court ordered appellate attorney. They handled filling an appeal. They must have grounds to file one, and in our case they had plenty of grounds. At first when I got the call by my attorney, a professional sounding woman, I was greeted by doubt and rejection in her voice. She didn't feel I had any means to file an appeal. "The CPS agency made a numerous amount of reports to the courts. And they were found to be true under the judge residing in your case. I don't see any leeway in filing for an appeal." She began... While she said all this, I felt a big drop in my soul. I couldn't believe I was hearing this terrible news. She didn't want to plead my case before the appellate courts. "I would need to review the evidence you submitted to the court. I have not received it yet. It was missing in the transcripts I received from the court's ruling. They were supposed to be included. I have already requested for them, so I should get them within a few weeks. But from what I have read so far, it doesn't look good. So if I decide not to take your case, you can always request for another appellate attorney. I just wanted to let you know." She offered me a phone number to other attorneys. I would hear from her soon. I was left with terrible doubt... I began to wonder what else could go wrong. I hadn't been getting any luck lately. My wife's encounter with her attorney had gone a lot more hopeful. The attorney was looking forward to filing an appeal, and was just waiting for the evidence as well. Apparently the court had neglected to attach documented evidence with the court's transcripts. Could this have been a simple mistake? Possibly... But it was highly unlikely. Who makes these kinds of mistakes? Someone would have to be very incompetent and lazy in order to make such a folly. But like I said, it was possible. But my suspicion was that this had been done deliberately. This would delay the appeal process, but it was not going to halter my hope to win.

Thanksgiving had passed and things were getting better between my wife and I. She was becoming more compassionate towards me, and beginning to appreciate all that I had done for her and Izabela. We had spent more weekends together at my cousin's house. My daughter was starting to develop a bond with me. She no longer cried when I held her. As a matter of fact, she would stop crying once I held her. (My wife was beginning to grow jealous.) I was so proud to show her to my family. My great grandmother, who still lives, was glad to meet her 4th generation offspring. My family were all delighted to see such a beautiful healthy baby in the family. I constantly held her, and responded to her baby cues. I could see that she felt safe in my arms. She could watch the world up close, and not feel afraid, from her daddy's arms... I was blessed to have her. And I knew that this was the way a father should treat his child... With love and kindness. She was getting spoiled by her two loving parents. But she deserved it. When the time came for them to leave and go home, it was always heartbreaking. My daughter would miss me. I could tell by the way she would stop smiling once she was strapped in the car seat, and noticed I wasn't coming. This had to be terrible for her. And I'm sure rather confusing. But it was something she would have to learn to understand later some day... I hoped she would understand. And I hoped it would not be too late. I constantly prayed daily for God to bring our

FAMILY BACK TOGETHER. I HATED THE FEELING OF BEING APART, AND I KNEW MY DAUGHTER WAS BEGINNING TO FEEL RESENTMENT EVERY TIME I WAS FORCED TO LEAVE HER. WE WOULD HAVE OUR CHANCE TO GET THE RESTRICTION REMOVED AT OUR 3 MONTH REVIEW COURT DATE COMING UP. AND I WAS LOOKING FORWARD TO IT.

THE DAY OF OUR PROGRESS REPORT I SHOWED UP TO COURT WITHOUT A LAWYER. I HAD FIRED MY LAWYER SHORTLY AFTER THE TRIAL HAD ENDED, SINCE I WAS NOT HAPPY WITH HIS SERVICES. NOR HIS BILL THAT HE SENT ME, FOR THAT MATTER. HE HAD CHARGED ME CLOSE TO 3 THOUSAND DOLLARS. (AND NOT ONE PENNY WAS WELL SPENT.) SO I DECIDED TO REPRESENT MYSELF, SINCE IT NO LONGER MATTERED WHAT HAPPENED FROM THIS POINT ON. THAT WAS THE WAY I SAW IT. I HAD LOST THE CASE AND WAS NOW UNDER THE MERCY OF THE COURT. WHAT GOOD COULD MY LAWYER DO FROM HERE ON, THAT HE COULDN'T DO BEFORE? MY HOPE WAS IN WINNING OUR APPEAL AND GETTING THE WHOLE CASE DISMISSED... THE APPEAL WAS GOING TO TAKE 6 TO 8 MONTHS. AS SOON AS COURT BEGAN, THE JUDGE ASKED ME ABOUT MY LAWYER. I INFORMED THE COURT THAT I WAS GOING TO REPRESENT MYSELF. THE JUDGE ADVISED AGAINST THIS, AND SET ME UP WITH A PUBLIC DEFENDER INTERVIEW. HE PROCEEDED WITH COURT, AND LISTENED TO THE PROGRESS REPORT WRITTEN BY THE CPS WORKER. IT WAS READ BY THE COUNTY COUNSEL, SINCE THE CPS WORKER WAS NOT PRESENT. BUT IN THE WORKER'S REPORT SHE WAS INSINUATING THAT I WAS BEING UNCOOPERATIVE. FOR THE MOST PART BECAUSE I LIVED IN ANOTHER COUNTY MORE THAN 50 MILES AWAY... WHICH, WAS A MATTER OUT OF MY HANDS. I WAS HOMELESS AND DEALING WITH IT AS BEST AS I COULD. OBVIOUSLY SHE DIDN'T UNDERSTAND THAT. THEY HAD NO REPORTS ON MY PROGRESS. "THE FATHER MOVED OUT OF THE HOME, AND GAVE UP HIS SECTION 8 VOUCHER TO THE MOTHER AND CHILD. THE FATHER HAS NOT BEEN IN CONTACT WITH CPS, AND THERE IS NO WAY TO REACH HIM. HE IS NOW LIVING IN ANOTHER COUNTY. THAT IS ALL THE PROGRESS WE HAVE FOR THE FATHER." THE COUNTY COUNSEL THEN GAVE HER REPORT ON MY WIFE, "THE MOTHER IS ADEQUATELY providing and taking care of her daughter. She attends all of her daughter's appointments, and the baby is thriving and healthy. The father has not been reported at any of the appointments. And there have been no complaints for the mother." This was the brief and extensive report. I asked for a chance to speak... "Thank you. I have not been able to attend any of the appointments due to my new location. I live very far, and I still don't have a car. I called the CPS worker before my phone was cut off, to let her know I moved out of the county. That is how she received this information. I do not have a contact number at this time, and I have not been able to afford one. I have been attending counseling in the town I live in, and have brought proof. I also have brought a copy of my psychological evaluation taken in August..." The judge cuts me off, and tells me "That's great. But you have to turn these into your CPS worker. You need to stay in direct communication with her, and let her know these things in order for me to know your progress. That's the way this works. I will not have time to review your evidence today, but give them over to the CPS supervisor and she will make copies for each of us present here. But it sounds like you're working on doing everything this court asks you, so let's hope it stays that way until our 6 month review coming up. Keep up the good work." Court was adjourned. We stepped in the hallway and met with my wife's lawyer. She gave us insight on how this progress review actually works. "This is a court date set up primarily for the judge to listen to the family's progress. The family is not given a chance to speak or file motions, or present evidence. They are just ordered to be present. But you guy's are doing a great job. Most parents don't have much to show in the first 3 month review. You practically have done everything the court has asked from you." She congratulated us for our hard work and dedication. But it still didn't ease my mind. I still couldn't go home and be with my family regardless of all my effort and cooperation. It was excruciating. I couldn't bear it much longer. I felt I

WAS REACHING MY BREAKING POINT... CHRISTMAS WAS RIGHT AROUND THE CORNER, AND I HAD BEEN HOPING THAT THIS WOULD ALL BE OVER. AT LEAST BE ABLE TO BE HOME WITH MY FAMILY. OBVIOUSLY DISAPPOINTMENT WAS BEGINNING TO BE AN EXPECTATION, AND MY HOPE AND FAITH WERE DOWN TO RAW BONE.

# TWENTY TWO

I WAS LOSING MY HOPE. MY FAMILY NOTICED THE CHANGES IN ME, MY LOW ENERGY, AND DEPRESSIVE MOOD. I WAS BATTLING WITH SUICIDAL THOUGHTS... BUT MY DAUGHTER KEPT ME FOCUSED ON STAYING ALIVE. I COULDN'T ABANDON MY PRECIOUS DAUGHTER... OR MY WIFE. MY WIFE TRUSTED AND DEPENDED ON ME SO MUCH. I WAS HER COAT IN THE WINTER, HER UMBRELLA IN THE RAIN, AND HER REFUGE THROUGH THE STORM. HER COMPASS IN LIFE. SHE CLUNG TO ME FOR DEAR LIFE. I WAS THE FIRST MAN TO SHOW HER LOVE, AND BRING HER HAPPINESS. I COULDN'T ABANDON MY FAMILY. THIS FIGHT AGAINST CPS WAS WEARING OUT MY SOUL. AND IT FELT AS IF GOD WASN'T LISTENING TO MY PRAYERS... I KNEW HE WAS THERE, BUT I STARTED QUESTIONING WHY HE WAS ALLOWING ME TO ENDURE SUCH LAWLESS WICKEDNESS. I COULDN'T THINK OF ANY SINS I HAD COMMITTED THAT WOULD RENDER SUCH CALAMITY. I CONSTANTLY REPENTED FOR MY SINS, AND TRIED TO ABSTAIN FROM COMMITTING FURTHER SIN. I COULD NOT UNDERSTAND WHY I WAS SUFFERING THROUGH SO MUCH PAIN. I THOUGHT WHEN YOU GOT SAVED AND GAVE YOUR LIFE TO CHRIST, THINGS WERE SUPPOSE TO GET BETTER. I DIDN'T LIKE THE WAY MY LIFE WAS BEING ABUSED, AND GOD DIDN'T SEEM TO BE RESPONDING. I WOULD SPEAK TO MY PASTOR AND OTHER CHURCH MEMBERS ABOUT IT, AND IT WAS ALWAYS THE SAME, "KEEP TRUSTING IN GOD. HE KNOWS WHAT HE'S DOING. MAYBE HE WANTS TO CHANGE YOU, AND MOLD YOU INTO WHAT HE WANTS YOU TO BECOME. HE HAS A PURPOSE FOR YOU. NOTHING IS BY COINCIDENCE." THEY WOULD ALWAYS TELL ME THE SAME RESPONSES. MY MOTHER TOLD ME THIS AS WELL. I HAD DECIDED TO GIVE HER A call, because I needed her help. The baby had been going to many appointments lately, and my wife's parents had stop letting my wife use their car. She would spend agonizing hours waiting for buses, and lifting the stroller onto the buses... We needed a car. I was hoping my mom would lend me money to buy one. I was due some back payments from disability, but I had yet to receive them. I would pay her back as soon as I received the check. "How much do you need? If you're going to buy a car make sure you have a mechanic look at it before you buy it. But I will do what I can to help you. God has put it in my heart to help you. I was praying the other day, and God told me to help my son." My mother's words brought me joy. Through her, God had revealed Himself to me and answered my doubts about His presence. He was confirming that He was still there, and that He was still with me. Helping me and constantly providing for me and my family. Despite of how bad the situation had grown to look. He was still there.

I had searched and searched for a car, and had settled on a particular brand. My wife had set her mind on that brand, was the real reason... A Lexus. (Like I said, my wife is spoiled and picky.) So when I found a sweet deal, I decided to surprise her. My cousin drove me to the meeting location, where the car owner and myself had decided on. When the owner pulled up, the car looked perfect. Just like in the pictures. The car wore 18 inch chrome rims, and had subwoofers in the trunk. And the motor ran very smooth and quiet... After all it was a Lexus. I was pleased with the vehicle, and handed the man the agreed amount in cash. I drove away in my new car. (It was new to me at least.) I was very thankful with God. He had blessed me with a great car, and I couldn't wait to see my wife's reaction. She was going to be very happy. I had bought the car for her and the baby. I was going to be too far away to take her and my daughter to her appointments, and I didn't want my daughter riding the bus any longer. So I had decided for my wife to keep the car with her, and the baby. I would just have to keep asking my family for rides for myself in the meantime. I didn't go out much anyways. I drove to my wife's and pulled into the driveway. She was surprised with my visit. She asked how I had gotten there. I took her by the hand and walked her to the car. She was taken by surprise, "You bought the Lexus! It's really nice babe. When did you buy it? Does it run good?" I unlocked the doors and let her in. I started it and turned on the music. "It has a sun roof! I love it. Mama's gonna love it too. Are you gonna let me drive it?" I began to laugh. She had so many questions, her mind was racing. "Yes babe. You can drive it. I bought it for you. And for the baby, so you guys don't have to ride the bus anymore." She was so happy (as I had expected) and she leaned over to give me a big hug and kiss. "Thank you Papa. I love it. Love you babe." We went and got the baby's car seat, and set it up in the back seat. We all went for a drive. I was in town, and I wanted to visit my relatives. But first I took my wife and daughter to a nice restaurant. This was a lot better than having to ride the bus. We could go where ever we wanted, and didn't have to spend hours waiting. We were both trying to take it all in. We hadn't had a car in almost a year. We were thankful for God's blessing... In the midst of all the chaos, heartaches, and pain.

# TWENTY THREE

Christmas had come, and we spent it together at home. I was in town, and we shared a home cooked meal. Courtesy of my wife's great cooking. We were working with what we had, and the food was delicious. Dinner and a movie... Just the three of us. We hoped next year would bring better times. But we were just thankful to be together. My cousins dropped by to visit. We all decided to go out for a night at the bowling alley. My wife had been complaining lately of staying home all the time, so it was going to be a good change in scenery for her... She needed that. I think all parents need that brush of fresh air from time to time. Newborns can be very time consuming. We played some arcades and bowled... My wife's best sport. The only game she can beat me in (just for the record). Well bowling and maybe basketball. But that's only because she's tall. (She's 5 foot 9 inches.) She beat me twice that night, and I won the last round. We are very competitive. Our games usually involve a lot of trash talking, and taunting. I felt sorry for our guests. After a long and exciting night we went home, and I spent the night at her house. I planned to spend the weekend with my wife and the baby. We were going to go to my cousin's house for new years, and she could drop me off then. The next morning my wife's cousin had sent her a text message and told her that she was in town. I had never met her cousin. Nor had I met most of her family. Her family wasn't very united or family oriented. They each did their own thing. Which is a lot different than my family. My wife had met almost all of my family (I say almost, because my family is so big) and she had grown fond of my family. She saw them as her family. She got along with everyone. And for the most part, they all liked her. She asked me if it would be ok for her cousin to come by and visit. I told her it was fine. I was looking forward to meeting her cousin. I have always wanted to be closer to her family. That's the culture I'm used to. Our family is very tight with each other. So it was a pleasure to have her cousin over to our house. I also wanted my wife to socialize, and get her mind on other things besides just taking care of the baby. It would be a good idea, and I welcomed it. Her cousin arrived a few hours later. My wife introduced us, and we shook hands. I was in the living room watching TV, and they decided to go into the bedroom and have "girl talk". After a while my wife returned to ask if it would be ok for them to go to the store. Her cousin wanted to buy Izabela some things for Christmas. I thought that was fine. She packed the baby's things and they left. I called my cousins and got them together to go out for the night. I was in town and I wanted to celebrate the holidays. By the time my wife returned with her cousin from the store, my cousins were at the house. I told my wife I was going to go out with my cousins. She was fine with it, and she told me her cousin wanted to spend the night. She could sleep in the guestroom. We both agreed, and I would come home later that night. Or at least I had planned to come home later that night, but there was a change of plans... My cousin had gotten a call from another one of our cousins (like I said, my family is big) and he was at a friend's house about 30 minutes away. So we decided to go out there. By the time I got home it was close to 7-am... My wife was furious. When I got home she was half asleep. The other half was waiting for me to get home. Her cousin had ended up spending the night, and they both had shared our bed. So I crashed out on the couch. I knew I was going to get an earful when I woke up... But I didn't think it would happen so soon. My wife threw a pillow at the back of my head, and told me to wake up! "Do you know what time it is? Wake up, I want you to help me with the baby." Her tone was angry. I was feeling hung over, and I couldn't move. I remained lying on the couch and finally fell back to sleep. I lifted my head up, just as she was walking out the door, "We're going to my cousin's house. I'll call you later." She yells out as she slams the door... I was tired and beat. I spent the afternoon sleeping.

By late that evening I started to wonder where my wife was. I hadn't gotten any missed calls, or texts from her. I texted her and she responded by telling me that she went to her cousin's house, because her cousin needed to get some things. I guess they had planned for her to spend another night at our house. I was ok with that. She said she would be home later. It was a bit humorous. I could tell she was still upset with me for coming home so late... This was her way of getting me back. She didn't tell me when she would be coming home. So I decided to get a hold of my cousins. I invited them over and we bought a few beers. A few hours had passed, and my wife still hadn't arrived. So we decided to go out to the pool hall. One of my cousins had his female friend drive us, since she was the only one that hadn't been drinking. When we got back my wife and her cousin had finally come home. They were in the bedroom when we arrived. We had brought a case of beer. We were each grabbing a beer, when my wife comes out of her room to see who's all in her home. She greets my cousins, and asks "What's this girl doing in my home?" She says out loud with rude attitude, and looking directly at her. "This is my cousin's friend from college. I just met her today." I told her. I asked my wife to please behave herself. Her behavior was embarrassing and inappropriate. I offered my wife a beer, and told her to let her cousin know she was welcome to drink as well. My wife went back into her room. A few beers had passed, and my wife would occasionally come out of her room to say a few smart remarks. Basically just to push my buttons, and ruin the fun. I could tell she was still mad from the night before... "You didn't even call me. I waited all night for you. My cousin had to see how you dissed me. Do you know how embarrassing that is? You're such a jerk!" Ouch... I'm sure my guests were happy to be a part of that wonderful exchange of words. I was extremely embarrassed. She didn't even give me a chance to explain, as she quickly walked away and went back into the bedroom. I was left with my guests and an awkward look on my face. "What was that about?" One of my guests uttered. I avoided the subject by walking to the fridge and grabbing some more beers. I would just have to talk to her later, when things were more appropriate and we were alone.

It started getting late and we were all becoming intoxicated. My wife had decided to join us in the living room, and was starting to loosen up. The alcohol was calming her anger. I noticed her cousin hadn't left the room the entire night. I decided to go talk to her myself, and invite her to join us. She was texting on her phone when I entered the room. "You're not drinking?" I asked her. She responds by showing me her bottle on the nightstand. It was almost empty. "There's more if you want some. You should come out and kick it with the rest of us. You're being a little anti-social." I tried to be nice and make her feel welcome. I hadn't gotten a chance to interact much with her, and so we hadn't gotten to know each other. So I was trying. She responded with a smile "I'm not anti-social, I'm just not dressed up to kick it. I'm in sweats and a T-shirt. You don't know me very well. I usually get all dressed up. But thank you." She politely rejected my offer. And I took it lightly. It was fine with me, I understood. "Well if you change your mind, you're more than welcome to hang out. It's just me and my cousins. One of them wants to meet you.

He's single." My wife came in the room while we were talking. I asked my wife to get her cousin to join us. "I tried telling her. But she doesn't want to. Why don't you want to come out? It's just his cousin. His other cousin and the girl left." My wife tells her cousin. I decided to leave the room, and see why my cousin had left. I guess it had gotten too late, and the girl had to work in the morning. So my cousin had left with her. My other cousin and I were left alone in the living room drinking. When my wife and her cousin came out of the bedroom, and sat in the living room with us. I offered them a beer and we all started to get acquainted. I introduced my cousin to my wife's cousin, and they began to conversate. I took the opportunity to talk to my wife, and ask her why she was being so rude earlier. I knew her reason, but I wanted her to know that it wasn't fair the way she was handling it. She didn't need to be so rude to my cousin and his friend. They had nothing to do with our relationship problems. She agreed that I was right, and that she shouldn't have acted the way she had. She began to laugh. She thought it was funny how she had been acting. The baby began to cry, and my wife went to go attend her. She was in her crib and had woken up hungry. So I went to the kitchen to make her a fresh bottle. When I returned I asked to hold my daughter, and I gave her the bottle. Soon she was fast asleep in my arms, and I took her to our bedroom. I had set up a bassinet next to our bed, since her cousin was going to spend the night in the baby's room (which we used as a guest room). I placed her in the bassinet and went back to the living room. My wife tells me that she's leaving... "What? It's almost 3 in the morning. Where are you going? No. You can't leave with the baby. You've been drinking. It's too late for her to be out. You can't go." I didn't agree with my wife going out at 3 in the morning. She was making a bad decision. My wife and her cousin had both been drinking, and it wouldn't be safe for the baby. "You can't tell me what to do. I'm gonna go spend the night at my cousin's." She tells me. She begins packing the baby's things, and her cousin was helping her. "You can't go. If you go then you can forget about me. We're done if you leave." I told her. I was hoping that she would take me seriously. "So you're gonna break up with me? You can be out till seven in the morning, but it's too late for me? You're so typical." She pushes me out of frustration. I bumped my back against the wall. Her cousin buts in and tells her "Just leave it at that. He said it's over, let's just go. Don't waste your time. He's not worth it." This had nothing to do with her, but now she had made it clear that she was the main instigator in my wife's behavior. Ever since she had gotten there, my wife had started to act different. I didn't like the negative influence she was having on my wife. I told her cousin to shut up. My argument with my wife had nothing to do with her. It didn't involve her. To this her cousin responded with, "I've had enough of this. I'm going to call the cops. Don't worry cousin the cops will help you." I was shocked... I also became worried. I became extremely angered by her threat. She wanted to call the cops so that I would have to leave and my wife could go out. My wife and I were having a simple argument, that hadn't even gotten loud or out of control, there was no need for police. My wife had pushed me, but it hadn't affected me. I didn't feel the need to call the cops. Why did the police need to be involved? My wife became upset with her cousin as well, and began arguing with her, "Don't call them. Why are you going to call them? He hasn't done anything. You know my situation. If you call the police, CPS is gonna get involved and they are going to take the baby from us. Why do you want to put me through that?" My wife tries to reason with her. But her cousin insists, "Don't worry. They're not gonna take the baby, they're gonna help you. Trust me." As her cousin says this, her cousin begins to reach down and picked up the baby from the bassinet. I rushed over to her and took my daughter from her hands. I placed my daughter on the bed, and told her cousin "Don't you ever put your hands on my daughter again! You are no longer welcome in my house. Now get the hell out!" I couldn't believe she was going to try to take my daughter. I told my wife in her cousin's presence, "Is this the type of people you let into our house? She wants to call the cops and bring more problems for our family. I don't want you speaking to her anymore. She's gonna make it impossible to beat the case now. They're gonna know that I've been visiting my daughter, and they're gonna want to put more restrictions on me. Thanks to your cousin. I don't want you talking to her ever again." My cousin comes into the room, when he hears the arguing. "What's going on" he asks. I told him what was going on, and what her cousin was trying to do, and that I didn't want her cousin in my house anymore. "Why are you gonna call the cops? My cousin hasn't done anything. They're just arguing. Like any other normal couple. Why do you want to call the cops, and make more of a mess for their family. They are trying to get their daughter back, and you're gonna make that harder for them. Haven't you ever argued with your boyfriend? Do you think it's necessary to call the cops because of arguing?" My cousin tells my wife's cousin. Her cousin began to cry. She felt like we were all ganging up on her. "I just want my cousin to be happy. Your cousin is controlling. He doesn't let her do anything, and now he's not gonna let her talk to me anymore. I need to call the cops. They're gonna help her. She needs to leave him. She can do better." She says. I think maybe she was a little too drunk. She was acting unusual, but like she had said, I didn't know her very well... I just wanted her to leave. She was trying to convince my wife to leave with her. To break up with me and have the police help her... It was ridiculous. My cousin took her to the living room to talk to her. He was going to try to convince her not to call the police. And explain to her that everything that was happening was between my wife and I, and to respect our relationship... But shortly after, he ran into the room and said, "She called the cops!" I rushed out the room and headed into the living room. A million thoughts were going through my head. She had now crossed the line, and was going to bring hell for me and my family. All the progress that I had made, all the effort to fight a corrupt system, and all my hard work to keep my family together was about to go down the drain. By one stupid phone call (that didn't even need to be made). I approached her and noticed she wasn't on the phone. She had the phone in her hand, but she was not on it. My cousin and wife were right beside me. "She called the cops, but she hung up." My cousin tells me. I began to yell at her to get out of my home. But she just stood there with a smirk on her face. My wife tells her "Why did you call the cops! Don't you know what that means? They're going to take my daughter away. Why are you doing this?" As my wife began to burst into tears, I grabbed the girl by her shirt. I grabbed her in a forceful bear hug, and began to drag her towards the door. "Get the hell out of my house! Don't you ever mess with my family again! I love my family. Don't you ever come back here!" I yelled at her, as I shoved her towards the door. My wife catches her as she almost falls, and helps her up. My cousin began to yell at me "Don't grab her like that. You could have hurt her. Let's get out of here, she's gonna call the cops. They're probably on the way." I couldn't believe this was happening. Why did I ever allow her into my home. Now I was forced to leave. If I stayed who knows what she was going to tell the police. That was her whole mission in the first place... To call the cops on me. Now my chances at moving back home with my family were obsolete. This was a nightmare inside of a nightmare.

## TWENTY FOUR

*Ring Ring*... I got a call from my CPS worker. She needed to speak to me, and said that it was urgent. She had received a police report from the night before. She wanted to ask me questions about what had happened. She said that I was involved in a fight, and that I assaulted someone. She wanted my side of the story. "Have you visited with Izabela since your last court date? Have you spent the night at your wife's home? I have a report that you assaulted some one in her home, and that you violated court orders. You are not allowed to visit Izabela without CPS supervision." She tells me. I began to answer her, "I have visited my daughter. I spend time with them, but I can't afford to go visit them all the time, because I live far away. But I've spent the night a few times at my wife's house. It was for the holidays." She cuts me off to add, "You are not allowed to live with your daughter! I can take your daughter away from you for this. You are not allowed to have contact with her without our permission or supervision. How many times have you spent the night?" She was extremely upset, and yelling. I answered her with, "I don't know how many times. I didn't know that I wasn't allowed to visit her. My lawyer told me I could. The judge never said that I couldn't visit her. The judge only said I couldn't live with them. I don't live with them, I only visit and spend the night sometimes, since it's far from where I live. I've only spent the night a few times. I don't know the exact number." She grew angered and shot back, "Well your lawyer is wrong! The court report says you can not have any unsupervised visits. I am going to have to put a temporary protective order. You are not allowed to go near her home. If you violate this protective order, we will have to terminate your rights and will take your daughter away! Do you understand? Can you promise me you will stay away from your wife and daughter?" She threatened to take my daughter if I didn't cooperate with her orders. Even though these CPS orders were not yet court ordered... But I knew the risks of going up against CPS... So I agreed, "Yes I can do that. I didn't know I couldn't visit them. I have been trying to get the restriction removed, I turned in all my paperwork to your supervisor. I have been waiting for your call. Did you get my paperwork?" She told me that she had received them, but that it wasn't enough to remove the restriction. "In order for me to remove the restriction, you must comply with the case plan and complete your counseling services. You must be addressing domestic violence issues through couples counseling, and you must be in contact with me. You and your wife are not involved in any couples counseling, so I cannot remove the restriction. When your doctor gives me proof that you no longer need services and have completed counseling I would be willing to discuss it with my supervisors. But right now you have more serious problems. You were involved in a nasty fight. Do you want to say anything about it?" She completely disregarded all the progress, and cooperation I was having with the courts orders. I had completed all the judges requirements and concerns... I was disappointed. I became worried about her persistent approach to find out what had happened the night before. From her comments I assumed there had been a police report made. "I wasn't involved in any fight. I haven't assaulted anyone. I don't know what your report says, but it isn't true. I'm not in any trouble. But I will stay away from my wife's home like you want me to." She wasn't satisfied. She kept asking questions. "I don't believe you. But

I will file my report to the courts and let the judge decide. You have to stay away from your wife and daughter from now until court. I am going to set up a new court date to deal with this issue. I suggest you follow my orders. I am not going to take your daughter away at this time. Your wife has been very cooperative, and has shown to be a good mother to Izabela. We will see each other in court."

I couldn't bear the new circumstances I was in. It was horrible... I lost my family again in an instant. The agency was going to file a restraining order against me, and there wasn't really anything I could do about it... My daughter belonged to the state. I was defenseless and impotent to the brutal force of the CPS agency. I hadn't assaulted my wife's cousin. I could only imagine the lies her cousin must have told the cops about me. Either way it was too late... My mind was filled with regret. I was in a low pit of despair, once again. My prayers were becoming muffled with the chaos... I could only ask for forgiveness. I hadn't intended to hurt that girl, but if I did I was sorry. My life was in God's hands, and He would judge me according to my sins. My repentance was sincere... In my misery I turned to drinking. And by New Years Day I had welcomed the New Year with a bottle of rum. I began to run from the things of God, and no longer wanted to hear about prayer or faith, or anything of that nature. I was returning to my old ways... Not caring. A life filled with sin. My hopes in a bright future were crushed. I could only see the dark abyss that engulfed me. It greeted me with open arms, and I gladly indulged. It was a friendly encounter... As if I was being reunited with an old friend. I turned my back on my wife and child. My wife would call me, and I would ignore the calls. I would speak harshly to her, without remorse or consideration... I didn't care anymore. I began to drift apart. I decided to look into moving far away. I wanted to get away from all the problems, and wanted to relieve my mind. Try to start new, and be stress free. I decided on moving to Mexico. I no longer trusted the United States government, and I was tired of being labeled a criminal within society. I was a victim of stigmas and racial profiling. I wanted to leave that negative stereotype behind... I had to if I wanted a chance at succeeding, and becoming someone in life. Be able to start a family without government intervention. Find a career and not have to go through the constant discrimination. I had made up my mind. I purchased a one way ticket to Mexico. Told my family I was leaving and left... My family, friends, and native land were left behind. My focus was on a better future... God willing.

# TWENTY FIVE

I couldn't stop thinking about my wife's sad look as I went through the airport security. My daughter didn't know what was happening. She was smiling and being her cute self. I kept thinking and visualizing them as I rode on the plane. I felt sadness, and countless thoughts of regret... If only I had done this or that different. Over and over, until I wore myself to sleep. Only to wake up as we were landing... "Beinvenidos a Mexico." I had arrived. I was glad to have landed safe. And I felt the change in atmosphere in my new homeland. The people were all brown like me. Families were joined together, and people were visiting or returning to beautiful Mexico. This was my first time to Mexico since I had been a child. (More than 20 years ago.) Once I gathered my bags and exited the security process, I was left waiting in the lobby. I exchanged some money to use the phone and buy some food. I called my wife... "Hey babe. I made it. I just wanted to let you know that I made it safe. It's nice here, the weather is good. I still haven't found out where I'm gonna go. I guess the hotels are only twenty dollars a night out here. So I'm gonna stay at a hotel until I find out how to get a hold of my family." My wife was glad to hear from me. She had been worried. "Thanks for calling. I've been praying that everything goes good for you. I hope you get a hold of your cousin that lives out there soon. At least the hotels are really cheap. That's good. Well keep in touch with me, and let me know how you're doing ok? I love you babe." She sounded sad. I was sure she missed me and hated the thought of me being so far. "I love you too" I replied.

Mexico is beautiful. The people are humble, and everyone is amiable. The atmosphere speaks loudly of the pride and essence of Mexico. I felt like I had been deprived my whole life from its beauty. I could only imagine the likelihood of my success, had I been exposed to a nurturing environment such as this. It was far from the oppression I was accustomed to in the United States. Laws and repercussions are the norm in the United States. The notion that American's are free, is far from true. I think the word freedom should be redefined, because my definition of the word does not fit to their truth. But maybe I'm miss-educated... I'm a high school drop out with only a GED. So I may be wrong, but I'm not too sure. But what I do know is that I have fallen in love with my ancestor's native land. I keep my wife updated, and keep in touch with her through emails. I provided her money through my bank account for her and the baby's needs. She informed me that the agency had filed a restraining order against me, and that since I wasn't in court they were also going to terminate my parental rights. "They wanted me to agree to the restraining order. They told me if I didn't agree to the restraining order, they would take Izabela. They said because if I didn't agree, I'm not showing a will to protect Izabela from you. They said that you're violent and that you assaulted my cousin. The judge made me agree to the restraining order. He said if I didn't he would take my daughter away. I didn't want to do it, but I was scared. I didn't want them to take her from us. I'm sorry babe." She confesses that she had agreed to a restraining order brought against me. I was not allowed to have any contact with my wife or child by protective order. Even though I hadn't assaulted anyone, or at least even been charged or convicted of assaulting anyone (much less my wife or child). The law hadn't issued any warrants, or pressed any charges. This was all being based on a police report made by my wife's cousin. And CPS jumped all over it, like a lion on its defenseless prey. "It's ok. I guess that's gonna ruin my record. Now I have restraining orders on my record. From my own wife and child, how do you think that looks? This is the whole reason I left the United States. I don't want to deal with their abuse anymore. How am I gonna get that off my record? I can't do anything about it now. Your cousin ruined everything. Thanks a lot." I was pissed. Things were continuing to get worse even in my absence. My wife began to cry. "It's not my fault. You always blame me for everything. I had to file the restraining order. They were gonna take Izabela. You weren't there. You left me here all alone. I have to deal with this all by myself. Sometimes I can't take it. I feel like I'm losing my mind." She confessed she'd been having a lot of anxiety and couldn't take it any more. She'd been taking her medicine, but I wasn't there to make sure that she was taking them on time. And to make sure that she didn't take more than she should. I told her to go visit my pastor. "You need to go to church. Go visit my cousin so you can go see the pastor. I'm sure she will let you stay the night there. You need to be prayed for. You're too stressed out. You need to get out of the house. It's all gonna be ok. Just call the pastor, and ask to go over there." She decided to take my advice and began packing. She had been going through a lot. She felt like she was all alone, and it was extremely hard for her. She was being forced to be responsible for a child all by herself. And she was hardly beginning to learn how to be responsible on her own... She was also upset with me for leaving her to go to Mexico. It was becoming unbearable for her. This whole melodrama had taken its toll on all of us... I was surprised that any of us were left standing.

After a few weeks had passed, things were starting to look a little better. My wife was getting more involved in church and spending more time with family members. Her mood was less agitated. I would call and make sure things were ok. My wife had received something in the mail for me, and told me it looked important. I told her to open it and to let me know what it was about... "It's from the police department. They are filing charges against you. They want you to appear in court next month. I think it has to do with my cousin. I think she's saying you stole her purse and beat her up." She reads me the letter and the charges. I was being charged with misdemeanor battery and petty theft... I couldn't believe it. I began to worry. I could end up in jail over this. This would mean that I now needed to return to California and fight the allegations. I didn't want to lose my disability income if I didn't respond to the charges. I would have to buy a ticket for next month, and make my way back to the US. I had gotten comfortable living in my new homeland, and I didn't want to return to the chaos of an over zealous government. But my choices were pre-determined. No matter what I did, I would eventually have to answer to the United States justice system. They would never allow something to slip out of from their rule and jurisdiction. The United States legal system is impeccable... Not in the aspect of justice, but rather in maintaining rules and punishment. The hands of the law are high strung on steroids! (It's an unfair fight.) So I will have to face the superior courts against my accuser, and hope for a fair verdict. My expectations are jail time and court fees. And of course new charges that would stain my record for the rest of my life. This is the norm for every American who faces the legal system, unless of course you are wealthy. In those cases there are compromises within the legal system, or rather a show of favoritism. But I am not fortunate enough to afford those compromises and must settle for the norm. I tell my wife not to worry. "Its ok. I knew this would happen. CPS has been waiting for this to happen. So that they could have something to use against me. I wouldn't doubt it if they're the ones instigating for the DA to press the charges. I'm just

GONNA HAVE TO DEAL WITH IT. I JUST DON'T KNOW HOW MUCH TIME I'LL BE FACING WHEN I GO TO COURT NEXT MONTH. IT DOESN'T LOOK GOOD." I HAD A PRIOR COUNT FOR GRAND LARCENY WHICH COULD ENHANCE MY JAIL TERM IF I WAS CONVICTED. I DIDN'T STAND A GOOD CHANCE WITH MY CRIMINAL HISTORY BACKGROUND, AND THE FACT THAT MY ACCUSER WAS A FEMALE DIDN'T HELP. JUST WHEN I THOUGHT THINGS COULD GET BETTER AND START NEW, I GOT PULLED BACK INTO THE DRAMA. WHEN WAS LIFE GOING TO CUT ME A BREAK... MY DISCONTENT AND ANGER STARTED TO TURN TOWARDS GOD. IN MY DRUNKEN BITTERNESS I BEGAN TO CURSE GOD FOR TURNING HIS BACK ON ME, AND FOR NOT PROTECTING MY FAMILY. ALL MY PAIN AND FRUSTRATION WAS TAKEN OUT ON HIM. I COULDN'T TAKE IT ANYMORE. I WAS TIRED OF PRAYING AND HAVING TO ENDURE SUCH HARDSHIPS. WHY WASN'T HE RUSHING TO MY AID... WHY? I WAS LOST IN A WORLD OF CHAOS. I FELT ALONE AND HELPLESS. I TURNED TO LIQUOR FOR SUPPORT... MY OLD BEST FRIENDS "JACK" AND "JOSE" (JACK DANIEL'S AND JOSE CUERVO).

# TWENTY SIX

My wife became difficult to get a hold of. She wasn't responding to any of my texts or answering my phone calls. I began to worry. I hadn't heard from her for a few days. I made several calls to close relatives and no one had heard from her. Her phone went straight to voicemail. I decided to call the CPS worker and ask about my wife and daughter. "I'm Izabela's father, and I'm calling to find out how she's doing. I can't get a hold of my wife, and I want to make sure they're ok." I told my worker. She answered me with "You are not allowed to have any contact with them. Have you been talking with your wife? You are violating the restraining order. You are not allowed to call them. If your wife has been talking to you she is in violation of the judge's order, and he may take Izabela from her care." She speaks in a devious and accusing manner. I tried not to let her get to me. I was not concerned with her legal tactics. "I'm concerned for my daughter. I want to make sure they're ok. I don't care about any order. I'm her father. The restraining order doesn't change the fact that she's my daughter. I want to make sure she's ok. Like any normal father would. Don't you have any children? I'm concerned for my daughter. That's all. Can you just tell me if you've talked to them?" I tried to emphasize with her, but to no avail. She responded coldly, "I cannot answer that. You need to worry about yourself. Your family is fine. Keep away from them. Where are you? I need to meet with you so that we can go over your case plan." She tried to persist me to meet with her, to go over her case plan for me. But I didn't have any plans to engage with CPS. My only concern was my wife and daughter at that moment. It wasn't usual for my wife to disappear, and I was worried about them. A lot of thoughts crossed my mind. My main concern was my wife's personal comments to me about being overwhelmed and taking too many pills lately. I was worried she might have overdosed. If she had, then my daughter could be all alone in the home unattended. I didn't want to expose my alarm to the worker. That would only make things worse. "I just want to know if she's ok. Can you just tell me that? I'm not involved in the case anymore. I thought you knew that. The judge terminated my services, so why do you keep insisting for me to meet with you? I just want to make sure my daughter is ok. That's all." I tried to make myself as clear and respectful as possible. But the lady just didn't budge. "I can't tell you that. I think it would benefit you if you were to meet with me. I know that you care for your daughter, and you want to be in her life. I can help you." Her words were distasteful... She was so full of crap. She didn't plan to help me. She wouldn't even tell me if my family was ok, or if she had talked to them recently. I decided to expose a little bit of my distress in order to get to the point... "My wife has been taking strong medication. I don't know if she took too many, and I want to make sure that she's ok. I want to make sure my daughter is ok. Can you tell me if you saw them recently? Or can you go and check on them and make sure?" I let her have the truth. I was more concerned with their safety than the repercussions. But I was not taken seriously. "What medications is she on? How do you know she's been taking these? I don't believe you. Do you have any proof? Your daughter is fine. Your wife is fine. You need to obey the restraining order and stay away from them. I suggest you meet with me. Can we set up a place to meet? I will meet you where ever you like." She completely ignored my concern and continued to persuade me to meet her. I was so disgusted with her and the CPS agency. I raised a valid concern in which my daughter may be at risk, and she completely ignored it. So I asked to speak to her supervisor. "She is in a meeting today, but I will give you the direct number to her voicemail." I decided to hang up on her, and I called the CPS hotline number instead. I stated to the receptionist my concern, and also explained my involvement in an existing CPS case. She asked me why I hadn't just called my worker and told her my concerns. "I did but she didn't listen to me. She was ignoring me. She didn't take me serious. I just want to make sure my wife and daughter are ok. Can you have someone check on them?" She would log my report into the system, and someone would follow up on it within the next 48 hours or so.

By the time my wife finally responded to my emails, my report had been made. She had responded with "I'm ok. The baby is fine." But that was about as far as she would respond. "I'm not supposed to be talking to you. You're going to make things worse. They think I'm abusing my medicine now. They forced me to live with my parents, so that my parents can supervise me. And I have to submit to random urine tests now thanks to you. Why did you call my worker?" My wife was upset. And she had a right to be. I had not intended for all that to happen. "I'm sorry babe. I was worried. You stopped talking to me. I didn't know what happened to you. I thought you might have took too many pills. Why did you just cut me off? Did you think I wouldn't worry?" I tried to explain how sorry I was, and tried to make her understand my concern. I was hundreds and thousands of miles away, I couldn't see what was going on, or know that nothings wrong. I was left with an unusual disappearance, and assumed the worst. "Well I'm not allowed to talk to you anymore. I don't want to risk it. This case will be over soon, and I need to beat the case without you making things worse. When this is all over we can all be a family again. But until then you need to just stay out there in Mexico. I don't want anymore problems from my worker. Don't write me anymore." My wife's final texts were heartbreaking... Her responsibility as my wife was being manipulated, and she was being turned against me. The CPS case was destroying my family at the core. By separating us and turning my wife against me. And my daughter was being stripped from her father's love. I decided to take an early trip back to the United States. I couldn't let my family be destroyed... Even if it meant I had to face the possibility of a jail cell.

# TWENTY SEVEN

As soon as I touched down on American soil, the feeling of vanity and racial indifference filled the atmosphere. People were rude and tended to be egocentric. It was the rude awakening that I was home... Back in the USA. I grabbed my luggage and took the shuttle to BART (Bay Area Rapid Transit). From there I took a cab to my wife's parent's house. I wanted to visit with my wife and see my daughter. I also needed to use my car. I knew my wife would be there. What I didn't know was that as soon as I knocked on the door, my wife's mother called the cops. My wife opened the door, "What are you doing here? You can't be here. My parents are going to call the cops. How did you get here?" She was scared her parents were going to call the CPS worker. She didn't want me to get in trouble. "Just leave. Please." She insisted. Her father had come to the doorway with a phone in his hand up to his ear. "I'M CALLING THE COPS. GET THE HELL OFF MY PROPERTY! YOU BETTER LEAVE BEFORE THEY GET HERE. THE COPS ARE LOOKING FOR YOU." He belts. He continued to threaten me as I tried to reason with my wife. "I just want to see my daughter. Do you see how your parents are? Let's go. Get the baby and get your stuff, and let's go. Your parents obviously don't want me here." I kept trying to convince my wife to let me see my daughter, but she just stood there looking helpless and scared. I hadn't ever seen her behave this way towards me... I was powerless. I asked my wife for my car keys so that I could leave. She came outside and handed me the keys. I placed my luggage into the backseat and asked her again to leave with me. But my wife kept refusing. She asked me to take a walk with her... "We need to talk, but not in front of my parents. Let's go for a walk. I don't know what's gonna happen now. The cops are gonna be here soon." As we were beginning to walk down the sidewalk, I looked back and saw her mother opening my car door. She was looking through my things. "Get the hell out of my car! What are you doing with my stuff!" I yelled. As soon as she heard me yelling at her, she got herself out of my car. She had been scrounging around in my backseat. When I rushed to close my door and lock the doors, she was standing next to the car pointing her fingers and yelling at me. I slammed the door and told her not to be going through my things. My wife's father, who was on the phone with the police, utters "HE JUST ASSAULTED MY WIFE. COME ARREST THIS GUY. I DON'T WANT HIM ON MY PROPERTY." The nerve of him... I hadn't even touched his wife. If anything I should be the one with the complaint. She was inside my vehicle without my permission. She opened the car door because I had forgotten to lock the doors. The chaos continued. Arguing back and forth, insulting one another. By the time the police arrived I was halfway down the block talking to my wife, and her father was still following us on his phone. I wasn't even on his property anymore, but he kept following us... It was pathetic. The cops asked for my ID and the usual police protocol. After much questioning the cops felt I needed to leave the area. They asked if I had somewhere else I could go. And I agreed to leave the area, I just wanted my wife to join me. But my wife's father kept insisting to the police that I had a warrant. But none showed up, because I had no warrants (I only had pending charges). This only made my wife's father more furious. He had expected to see me arrested. So he asks to speak to one of the police officer's alone. He gives me an evil look and says "GET READY. BECAUSE YOU'RE GONNA GO TO JAIL TONIGHT." I just laughed at his angry demeanor. He was so hell–bent on sending me to jail. The guy hated my guts. He wasn't going to give up on the fact that I wasn't going to jail. The officer left to go speak to my wife's mother. When the officer returned, I was placed in hand cuffs and placed under arrest. My wife started yelling at them, "Why are you arresting him? He hasn't done anything. What did you tell them Dad? Why are you doing this? What did Mom say to them?" My wife was in tears and torn between her parents and her husband... While I, was being sat in the backseat of a police car. "What am I being arrested for?" I asked the officer. "You're under citizen's arrest." He said. I didn't quite understand what that meant or why it was happening. So I asked him what that meant. "It means someone has made a complaint about you, and they want you arrested. It's called a citizen's arrest. You're being charged with battery." This was just great. I had barely arrived to the United Stated, and this was what I had come home to... So much for a "welcome home" party. I couldn't believe I was being arrested for something I hadn't done. And to have her mother lie to the police was just insane. The things people do when they hate someone, is just unbelievable. It wasn't enough for them to get my daughter taken from me through CPS, now they were sending me to jail... I would have to sit in jail and wait for my wife to bail me out. I didn't want to stay in jail. The officer opened the window so I could speak to my wife before he drove me to the county jail. She was sorry that this was all happening. She apologized for her parents accusations. "You shouldn't have came. I knew this was gonna end up bad. Now the CPS is gonna make more restrictions. Why did you come here? I gave the police my statement. I told them you never hit my mom. I don't know why my parents are doing this. I can't see you anymore. Not until this is over. Please understand that." She was doing what the CPS wanted. She didn't want to lose the baby. I had to learn to understand that... I was completely torn apart on the ride to jail. I couldn't believe that I would spend that night in jail. I had been hoping to see my daughter and spend time with them. I had been gone for so long... But now reality set in. And I was being booked into the county jail.

After 72 hours, I was released from the county jail. The charges had been dropped. The alleged incident, that was never filed, my wife's mother had said I pushed her. This had been the accusation that had lead to my arrest. That's how unfair the legal system is. My witness' testimony on the scene wasn't enough to not arrest me, but it was enough for the DA not to file charges (petty charges at that). So I had spent almost 3 days in jail over a bogus accusation, even though I had never pushed my wife's mother. And I've never even heard of anyone going to jail for pushing someone. When I wound up in jail my life had finally hit rock bottom. My desire to live had ceased. I had begun to contemplate suicide... And I was dead serious. When I got out of jail I wanted to end my life. I went to the liquor store and bought a fifth of tequila. I took it back to my place and commenced to drowning myself in alcohol... Halfway through the bottle I became angry. I was mad at the world. I hated how my life had ended up... I was mad and disappointed in myself. I wound up staring face to face in the mirror... And I began to punch vigorously at the closet mirror. I pounded until the closet became bits and pieces. I even continued stomping the bits of glass on the ground, and made them mush in the carpet. I then took up a blade of glass in my hand, and began to slash at my arm. Deep cuts ran up my arm... The blood was thick, dark and red. Drops of blood stained the carpet floor. My shirt and pants were drenched. But I was still alive. I was not yet satisfied... I laid on the floor drunk and bleeding. I was torn apart inside. I cried out to God with tears down my face... I cried myself to sleep. I would have to find a better way to end this misery.

The CPS agency had been notified of my arrest, and had petitioned for another restraining order. The prior protective order was only valid for 30 days. Since I had never been formally served the restraining order to show up in court, and therefore the restraining order had been dropped. That's why I was not in any violation when I showed up to my "in-laws" house, and the police had no reason to arrest me. But of course this did not satisfy my wife's parents, and that's when they proceeded to have me arrested by any means... Even by lying. The agency had been contacted (and I'm sure by my wife's parents as well), and they were requesting a new restraining order. The next few days I spent talking to my brother and my cousin over the phone. I talked to them about how I was feeling. I told them about the incident the night before, where I had tried to kill myself. They didn't want me to hurt myself. My cousin was upset with me for cutting my arm, and for trying to end my life. My brother kept telling me not to give up. He didn't want to lose his oldest brother. I was the one he had always looked up to when we were younger, and now I was giving up on life... He didn't want to accept that. "You're better than that. You need to stick around for your daughter. This is all gonna pass, things are gonna get better bro. I know you don't see it now, but it is. We love you man, don't do nothing stupid. I'll fly over there if I have to. I don't want to lose you bro. Do you want me to go with you to court, so that I can tell them how much of a good father you are? Because you practically raised me. I can take time off school to go help you." My brother was insisting to help me, as long as I would agree not to hurt myself. We had grown up without a father, my Dad had died when I was nine. I was the oldest of 3 brothers... I told him I would like for him to come visit me. I hadn't seen him in over a year, and needed his support. Times were extremely hard, and I felt alone. "Alright bro. I will get a plane ticket as soon as I find out from my school, if they will let me take some time off. If not I'll just retake the class next semester. I will let you know as soon as I find out. I will probably be out there by next weekend. Just hang in there. Everything's gonna work out. Just give it some time. I'm gonna see you soon. Love you bro." My brother would be flying out to see me the following week. He wanted to talk to the CPS judge on my behalf. He knew how much it was affecting me, not being able to see my wife and daughter. He wanted to explain to the judge that I was not a danger to my daughter or my wife. I didn't think it would help much, but it was worth a try. At least I would get to spend time with my brother. My other brother wanted to come and visit as well, but his job and responsibilities were too much for him. So he wouldn't be able to come out and see me this time... but hopefully soon.

# TWENTY EIGHT

It had been a long time since I had seen my brother. I noticed he had gotten bigger. My little brother had been working out lately... He wasn't so little any more. He was actually larger than me. He gave me a hard time about this. It was playful humor between brothers, and I didn't take offense to his jokes. We spent the afternoon together, and I showed him around the town. He hadn't been in California for a few years. We met up with other relatives later that night, and did a lot of catching up. He was glad to be home... California is our birth place. My brother was eager to meet his niece. He hadn't gotten a chance to meet her yet. My daughter would be turning one in about a week... A whole year had gone by since she was born, and I still hadn't gotten a chance to enjoy God's blessing. This was the root of my depression and bitterness. My brother called my wife to try to set up a chance to meet. But my wife was not sure if her father would allow that. She didn't want any problems at home. She was still living under her parent's roof, and she was under their control. My brother would have to wait for court, same as me, to get to see Izabela. The court date was scheduled two days before my daughter's birthday. And I was hoping God would allow me to see my daughter on her special day... It meant a lot to me.

I decided to take my brother to church with me on Sunday. And he agreed to join me. I had been waiting for the opportunity to bring my brother to church, and finally the chance had come. When we arrived I introduced him to some of the brothers in Christ that I knew. We took our seats, and I began to pray. As the music from the choir filled the church, I could feel God's presence. I had a huge burden that I was carrying on my shoulders, and I needed God's help. My spirit yearned for His mercy and His love. As the sermon went on, I could feel the message touching my soul... God had begun to speak to me through the words of the pastor. I was filled with Gods love, and His Holy Spirit. After the service I went up to the alter, and my brother followed me. As I was being prayed for by the brothers from church, I felt a peace come over me. I then watched as they prayed over my brother, and he gave his life to Christ. I was very proud of him. I had been waiting for this moment for a while... And it had finally happened. At that moment God had answered one of my prayers. A prayer I had made when I became a Christian. I had prayed for my family to be saved... And here I was seeing it happen. God is faithful to His word. And I thank God for His salvation.

When it was time for my protective order hearing, I showed up to court with my pastor, my brother, and my teacher from the counseling training program I had been attending before I dropped out. They had come to show support, and to express their discomfort with the judge and the CPS agency. They didn't agree with the way I was being treated. And they didn't like what was being done to my family. I had explained to my pastor how I had lost my hope, and wanted to give up on life. But he kept telling me to trust in the Lord... "How can I trust Him, when I've been putting my trust in Him and He doesn't help me? I've tried to have faith. I've been praying and trying to do what's right, but nothing works. I can't take it anymore. It's useless. No matter how much I pray, things just keep getting worse. I already know that the judge is not going to drop the restraining order. I'm not gonna get to see my daughter on her birthday." I expressed my frustration and doubts to my pastor. But he did not agree with what I was saying. He told me to keep trusting in God. And that I needed to have faith. He told me that I'm wrong in my way of thinking, and that I needed to learn to trust God. That this was just a part of tribulation, and that I needed to build my faith. God wanted to mold me to be how He wanted me to be... But I didn't want to hear this. My pastor didn't seem to understand all that I was going through, and how long I had been suffering. "I need help here. I'm drowning in all these problems, and instead of Him reaching His hand to help me, He pours more problems. I don't know how that is supposed to help me, but this is too much for me. I just want a normal life. I don't deserve all this. I don't want any more problems. I need Him to help me." My exhaustion was sincere. And I could not stand for any more problems. I was at my lowest point. I was a fraction from my breaking point... I wanted God to see that, and cut me a break. I would have to wait for God to respond.

We sat in the court lobby for several hours. We had been scheduled for a court hearing at 9–am. And it was now close to 4–pm! I was outraged and extremely impatient. My wife out of fear for the agency, decided not to bring my daughter. She had left her at home with her parents. She didn't want the CPS agency to find a reason to keep reprimanding her. And if she brought my daughter, she knew I would have been trying to hold her and be with her. The agency might have tried to make that an issue, since I was not allowed to have contact with my wife or daughter. So she decided not to bring her, to avoid anymore problems from CPS. She even chose not to sit by me, or have any contact with me, out of respect for the restraining order being sought in place by CPS. My pastor had to leave early. We hadn't planned to be in court all day, and he had to leave around 1 o'clock. But I thanked him for coming to help... Things hadn't looked hopeful from the start. I was going through the court motions, but I knew that there was no point in fighting the case anymore. The judge would do as he pleased. This was the same judge that felt my daughter needed to be taken and protected against me. His views and opinions seemed corrupted and vile. I couldn't stand to be in his courtroom any longer... This would be my last appearance. If God wouldn't answer my last request to be free to see my daughter and visit her without restrictions, I planned to blow my brains out... And only God could judge me. Our case was finally called into the courtroom. We took our places, and my visitors were asked for their names by the court clerk. As the judge began, he started with "We don't have much time, so we are going to try to make this quick. We have about 15 minutes. So let's try to finish by then." He tells everyone present as his focus is on the clock on the wall. I began to see the outcome in my mind. I knew 15 minutes was not enough time to argue my case. This was a hearing that CPS had petitioned for a restraining order. Obviously the judge planned to grant it in 15 minutes flat... That seemed to be the case. I don't know why they even bother with due process of law. They should just do away with it and let judges rule without any facts other than police and state official's reports. It would save tons in wasted tax payer dollars... As well as wasted time. Due process is such a farce. The county counsel spoke on behalf for the CPS agency's petition, and she took up the majority of the time left. By the time I was left with a chance to speak, the judge cut me off. "Well it looks like this is going to take longer than what we expected. Let's reschedule for a later date. In the meantime I will keep the temporary protective order in place." I was left without the chance to fight the restraining order, and be given the chance to see my daughter freely. Izabela's birthday was coming up in two days... I already had the feeling that it would be impossible to win this hearing. And once again

God had left my prayers unanswered. It made me sick to my stomach. I spoke out and cut the judge off. "My daughter's birthday is on Wednesday. I've been waiting all day since eight thirty this morning to get this restraining order removed. I want to be able to see her on her birthday." I told the judge, and the whole courtroom stopped. They hadn't expected for me to speak, much less out of turn. But frankly I didn't care for their ridiculous formalities. "Well if the county counsel doesn't object, I think we can make an exception. In the past you were not open to setting up for a supervised visit. Would you be willing to visit with your daughter under the agency's supervision?" He asks me directly. At the judge's request, I decided to lower my high expectations to the mere ability to visit my daughter for an hour under CPS supervision. I had made it to that low point in my life, and my only focus was on the chance to spend time with my daughter for her first birthday... I would take what I could get. I agreed to the opportunity he was granting me (as mediocre as it was). The judge gave his final orders, and I was granted a supervised visit for April 8th, 2009. My brother stood up and asked for a chance to speak. "Who are you?" The judge asks him. "I'm his brother. I flew out here to support my brother. He's not a bad person. He's not the way they're making him seem. He loves his daughter, and he's trying to be a good father. I know he's going to be a good father, because he helped raise me and my brother when we were young. He's a good brother. I think if you guys give him a chance you will see that." He was interrupted by the judge "I thank you for your input. But this court has run out of time. Perhaps you would like to be at the next court hearing. I am going to adjourn this meeting, if county counsel has nothing further." The court was adjourned. We had gone about 20 minutes over the time limit, and the judge was eager to leave. He probably needed to go home to his wife and children. Something I was not fortunate enough to have an

OPPORTUNITY TO DO... I WAS LEFT HOMELESS, AND WITHOUT EVEN THE CHANCE TO SEE OR SPEAK TO MY FAMILY.

# TWENTY NINE

I was a wreck. The restraining order had left me without any hope. My faith was gone. There was no point in reviving something that was dead. It was overkill. I took my defeat bitterly, like a shot of tequila. I rushed home and decided I would load my .357 magnum... When I got there, my pistol was missing. Someone had taken it, and the only one who knew about it was my brother. He had deliberately hid it from me. He knew my intentions and the goal I had set in my mind... I wanted to end my pain. I was furious... "Where is it? Why did you hide it? You can't stop me. I can get another one. Just give me my gun and let me deal with my problems on my own. I don't need you making more problems for me. Do you like to watch me suffer? Why are you getting in between my problems? You're not helping me." I told my brother to just give me the gun. He couldn't stop the pain I was going through. He couldn't solve my dilemma... As much as he wanted to help, he was only making things worse by forcing me to face my living hell. I wanted to rest at peace finally... Even, if it meant pulling my own trigger. What more did I have left to give? I was spent and exhausted. I needed to rest my mind. What was wrong with that? My brother began to tear up. "I can't let you do that. I love you bro. I don't want to live without my older brother. I look up to you man. How do you think we're going to live the rest of our lives knowing that you killed yourself? How do you think our Mom is going to feel? How about your daughter? Don't you think she's gonna want to have you in her life? We know what it's like to not have a dad. Do you want that for her? I can't let you do it man. Even if you get mad at me. I wouldn't be able to live with myself, knowing that I gave you back your gun. I know you're going through a lot. But you can't give up. You told me to believe in God, and I got saved because of you. Now you're giving up, and saying that God doesn't help you. So should I stop believing in God too? If He doesn't help you, then why should I trust Him?" My brother's sadness brought tears to my eyes as well. He compelled me to give up the thought of ending my life, as I began to feel guilty. I didn't want to be the reason for my brother to stumble in his new walk with God. My failures should not be his stumbling blocks... My example should serve as stepping stones for him. Not cause set backs in his relationship with God. But in my misery, I had let my problems get the best of me, and win my faith... I was drastically losing this battle. I prayed to God and asked God for His forgiveness... I made an agreement with my brother, and decide to give life another try. I would give it more time. The circumstances had become unbearable, and I was reacting impulsively. I needed to take it one day at a time, and just trust in God... As difficult as it seemed, I had no other choice. And in the meantime, I looked forward to seeing my daughter for her birthday.

I had bought mija an elmo doll and book for her birthday, some dresses and clothes. I called the CPS worker early in the morning to set up the visit. I left her a message and waited an hour... I called again and left another message... After an hour and a half I tried the number again. By Noon I decided to go down to the social services building in person instead, along with my brother. We enter the building and headed to the floor where they held supervised visits. I asked the receptionist if they had my name on the list, but she didn't have me listed. "Who is your worker?

Do you have a visit for today?" She asks me. I was confused and beginning to get upset. I tried to remain calm, "I was court order a supervised visit for today. I've been calling my worker all morning." The receptionist asked for my worker's name and looked her up. She called my worker and spoke to her. After a short conversation they hung up. "Your worker is going to be giving you a call right now. I told here you're here. But she says that she hasn't made a reservation." The receptionist shares briefly with me her conversation with my CPS worker. It was upsetting... I had been calling her all morning and she still hadn't returned my calls. Yet here was a fellow employee calling on their business line, and she was quick to answer. I knew that the worker was purposely avoiding me. The receptionist adds, "Your worker needs to make the reservation before 3-pm if you want to get a visit. We're all booked up. Three o'clock is the last available slot." She advises me to hurry with my reservation. And just then my worker calls my phone... *Ring Ring* "I received your calls this morning, but I have been very busy today. I will be in court for most of the day today with another case. You should have called me yesterday. I can try to set up a visit for tomorrow. I will give you a call tomorrow to set it up." My worker easily avoids the fact that she has been avoiding me all morning, by claiming to have been busy. And completely ignores the fact that I was court ordered a visit for today. I responded briskly, "I've been calling you all morning. I've been waiting for your call. But that doesn't matter now. I'm here at the visitation. I need my visit today, I was court ordered a visit for today, not tomorrow. My daughter's birthday is today, not tomorrow. I brought gifts and my family here today to visit her. I don't want a visit tomorrow. And I don't care if you're busy, send someone else to fill in for you. I don't need you to supervise me. I'm sure you can find someone else to do it for you. Just like you have your co-workers sit in when you're out of the office. And I didn't call you yesterday because I didn't have to. You could have called me if you needed to talk to me. You got the court order Monday, you had all day yesterday to set up the visitation. You have a job to do, so do your job." My tone was harsh, and my mood was firm. I was done being shoved around by their every whim. I needed to enforce the court order that was in my favor, just as they enforced every order that was in their favor. I was granted a petty hour visit for Mija's birthday, what was the problem with fulfilling the court's order in my favor? The worker was intentionally being malicious. "I have to be there, I'm sorry. Please understand that it takes time to set up visitation. I did not have enough time to reserve a slot for today. They are very busy today, and there are no more rooms available. I can set up a visit for tomorrow. I need to give your wife prior notice to give her enough time to bring your daughter to the visit." She refused to have someone else supervise me. And she tried to lie about the visitation being full. "I talked to the receptionist and she said they have an opening at 3 o'clock. I'm court ordered a visit, so are you not going to obey the court order? But you expect me to follow the court orders?" I couldn't believe I was even dealing with this. I had lowered myself to a supervised visit, and now I wasn't even getting that... I looked at my brother. He was silent. He knew what I was thinking. One thing after another, it just never seemed to end... I was only trying to see my daughter. I had decided to keep trusting in God, and now this. What's going on here... "Why do I keep going through this Lord?"

I was denied the chance to visit my daughter... Happy Birthday Izabela. The CPS worker told me to give her a call the next day to set up a visit. I drove home defeated. I was left speechless and lost for words. I had been looking forward to holding my daughter. Kissing her and seeing her beautiful smile... It would have brought my soul a bit of joy. Instead I was seeing the flash of red and blue. The cops were pulling me over... "License

AND REGISTRATION. KEEP YOUR HANDS WHERE I CAN SEE THEM. DO YOU KNOW YOUR TAIL LIGHT IS OUT?" THE OFFICER HAD PULLED ME OVER DUE TO MY TAIL LIGHT BEING OUT. HE WENT BACK TO HIS CAR TO RUN MY INFORMATION, AND BY NOW I KNEW I WAS GOING TO JAIL. I HAD MISSED COURT FOR THE BATTERY AND PETTY THEFT CHARGE THE DAY BEFORE, BECAUSE I HAD SHOWN UP TO COURT LATE. I DIDN'T KNOW WHAT TIME I NEEDED TO SHOW UP TO COURT, BECAUSE I NEVER HAD RECEIVED THE LETTER. MY WIFE HAD THE LETTER, BUT I WASN'T ABLE TO HAVE CONTACT WITH HER, SO I DIDN'T KNOW WHAT TIME I HAD COURT. SO WHEN I GOT TO COURT, I WAS LATE AND THE JUDGE HAD ALREADY ISSUED A BENCH WARRANT. BUT I HAD PUT MYSELF BACK ON THE CALENDAR, AND HAD A COURT DATE FOR THE FOLLOWING DAY. BUT UNFORTUNATELY I WAS BEING PULLED OVER FOR A ROUTINE TRAFFIC STOP... A BURNT TAIL LIGHT (JUST MY LUCK). "STEP OUT OF THE VEHICLE, HANDS ON YOUR HEAD! YOU'RE UNDER ARREST." THE COP CUFFED ME AND SAT ME ON THE CURB. I TRIED TO EXPLAIN THE SITUATION, AND SHOW THE PROOF I HAD FROM THE PUBLIC DEFENDER'S OFFICE SHOWING MY UPCOMING COURT DATE. BUT IT WAS TOO LATE. THE BENCH WARRANT HAD BEEN ISSUED. AND I WAS GOING TO SPEND THE NIGHT IN JAIL... I WOULD HAVE TO ACCEPT IT. APRIL 8TH 2009 WAS SPENT BEHIND BARS. IT WAS MY DAUGHTER'S FIRST BIRTHDAY. AND HERE I WAS, GOING THROUGH OVERWHELMING OBSTACLES... I WAS SO DETACHED THAT FOR THE LIFE OF ME I COULDN'T MUSTER A TEAR... I WAS NUMB, BUT MY SOUL WAS DYING INSIDE.

# THIRTY

I was escorted into the courtroom, handcuffed and wearing county blues. I looked guilty as sin. That is what every inmate looks like, when presented in this menacing attire. My many tattoos doesn't help in my defense... No matter what the charges may be, the tattoos and skin color always make me appear guilty. I was read my charges, and my public defender pleaded for my release from custody. The judge was weary to release me to the public. My arrest record is extensive, and a judge is never satisfied when responding to such. My lawyer spoke in my defense. "My client was arrested for the bench warrant that you issued two days ago. He had presented himself to court on that earlier court date, but had arrived late for his arraignment. He went down to our public defender's office himself and put himself back on calendar. This is the court date he was given. Unfortunately he was pulled over yesterday for a minor traffic violation and was taken into custody. My client has not shown any indication to flee from prosecution. He has shown the opposite. He has presented himself to court, and is willing to fight the allegations from the complaining victim. I request that you 'OR' my client. I don't see a reason why this court shouldn't. The charges are misdemeanors in this case. And my client is willing to present himself to his future court dates." As the attorneys made their arguments to the judge, the DA was marking me as a threat to society. But the judge agreed to release me, under the statutes of the law. And I was granted OR (own recognizance). If I failed to appear in court for future court dates, I would be taken into custody... I did not plan to miss my court dates. I was very relieved to be able to get a chance to be out of custody. I didn't think that the judge was going to do that for me. But when he did, I felt maybe God was beginning to help me. And it made me feel better to know that God didn't leave me in jail. I was later released that day, and when I got out I was contemplating what to do. Everything was so bent out of shape, and my life was in total ruins. I didn't know where to go, or who to turn to. My cousin in San Diego learned about my release, and offered to help me out. "Why don't you come out here and visit. I'll show you around out here. You can get away for a while and just hang out. It'll be cool bro." My cousin had been wanting me to go see him for some time. Because of the distance, it had not been easy to stay in touch. I decided to take him up on his offer. I looked at it as an opportunity to get away from the drama, and try not to focus on the upcoming trial and possible jail time.

San Diego was a nice change in scenery. The beautiful coast, and elegant buildings made a pleasant view. Palm trees and granite landscaping. High end model vehicles seemed to be the norm. I was taking it all in, and appreciating the beauty. We spent the weekend barbecuing and drinking coronas. I avoided thinking of my problems, and felt refreshed for once. My cousin drove me around town, and showed me the popular areas. He had joined the Navy many years ago, and had been stationed in San Diego for a while. He was very familiar with his new city. My time in San Diego was well spent, and it helped me renew my desire to live. I began to hope for a better future. When it was time for me to leave, I was grateful with my cousin for having me over. We had bonded and caught up on so much time apart since our youth. We had grown up in the Bay Area as teenagers. We were now men, caught up in our daily lives. Our childhood was a distant memory. But it was nice to reminisce and regain that camaraderie. On my way back to the Bay, I made a stop in LA to visit with my tia. My tia had moved out to LA recently, and I hadn't seen her in a few years. My little cousins had grown a lot and were getting older. I was glad to spend time with them. We all talked over dinner together, at an authentic restaurant. My little cousin talked about his new girlfriend... He was only 10 years old. And I thought this was hilarious. His girlfriend was 12. There were many new stories that were funny. And some that were shocking. But all in all it was a pleasant visit. We agreed to keep in touch and said our goodbyes. My aunt would be praying for me. She didn't want me to go to jail. She knew I was staying out of trouble, and was concerned for me. I faced a hard reality... But I was just letting life have its way. God would decide my fate. I was done fighting for my fate. God had the final say.

# THIRTY ONE

Day in and day out, I was constantly fighting my charges. Trial had started, and I was busy picking a jury. The process was a long one. There were 49 potential jurors. Each potential juror had to go through an extensive background and mental examination. It was an elimination process. I was not surprised to have the majority of jurors involved in law enforcement. Many were retired military and associates of the police department. I did not see how this was being a fair procedure. This was supposed to be a jury of my peers, but the jurors were not even close to such. Many were in their forties plus... That was a huge generation gap. I just worked with my options, and dismissed the bad candidates. It was like plucking weeds from the yard. There were many weeds... And it was frustrating. By the second week of having court everyday, I had become familiar with the faces of everyone in the courtroom. And we had finally reached a jury. It was made primarily of women... Nine women and three men. We were ready to begin the trial. My wife's cousin had appeared in court, and took her place on the stand. She would testify, under oath, the incident that took place 6 months ago. I braced myself for the lies she would swear on the witness stand. This was going to be humiliating... I could only imagine how this was going to turn out. She ultimately began by crying after only two questions... Sobs and tears were the intro for the case. It was a very dramatic entrance. And it caught the juror's sympathy. And instantly their dissatisfaction turned on me. I could feel their heavy gazes in my direction... I became very uncomfortable. I was like a scapegoat, or the target of a roast session. I was being attacked by every false statement she made. And the DA pressed on her ever word, trying to gain the jury's sympathy. He manipulated their anger towards me... He even pointed directly at me as he spoke harsh accusations. I could only sit their, and refrain from speaking in my defense... "I was scared for my life. I didn't know what he was going to do. My cousin and him were arguing. I wanted to leave. I didn't feel safe. I was going to pick up the baby, but he pushed the baby back on the bed and started cursing at me. He told me to never touch his daughter, and then he hit me." She started to cry again, and the DA brought her tissue. It was very intense. She had made a version that put me in an awful position. As if I went around hitting women, and even pushing my own daughter... It was disgusting. She continued with her story. The DA asked if she could remember if the baby was hurt by the push, and if she could describe where she was hit. "The baby wasn't hurt. She was ok. She just laid there. I think she started crying, I'm not sure. He hit me on top of the head really hard. I don't remember which hand he used. I just remember that it hurt. After he hit me, I tried to leave the room to call the cops. I was going to call the police, but someone hit the phone out of my hand and it hit the floor. And the battery fell out." She started to make it seem as if she was running for her life, and needed to call the police. But apparently "someone" had knocked the phone out of her hand... The DA asked if she knew who hit the phone out of her hand. "I don't remember. I had my back facing them, and when I put the phone to my ear someone slapped my arm and the phone hit the floor. I didn't see who did it. But when I turned around he was the one standing closest to me." She was implying that I possibly hit the phone out of her hand, but she was not sure. She didn't see who hit the phone out of hand, but I was standing directly behind her when it took place. This of course never happened, but it was a great description of events. And her main objective was to convict me. At the moment she was winning the battle... Things were not looking good. She continued with her allegations. "When the phone got hit out of my hand, I was in the living room. I turned around and he was right there. His cousin and my cousin were right behind him. He then grabbed me and began choking me. He choked me until I blacked out. When I woke up I was on the ground, and he was on top of me. Yelling at me and hitting me in my stomach. His cousin was pulling him off of me. I heard his cousin tell him, I told you not to be doing that. And then they ran out of the house." She ended her statement by crying uncontrollably. The DA asked the judge for a short recess. "Your honor, the victim has had to relive this tragic event. I think it would be a good time for a short recess. So that she can take a moment to regain her composure. Out of respect for the victim, I'm sure we would all agree." Court would take a 15 minute break. The weight of her testimony was thrown on my shoulders. I couldn't imagine winning after her brutal testimony... It was going to be extremely unlikely. I didn't even bother praying anymore. I had given that up a few weeks ago. I had decided to leave my life in God's hands. Regardless if I prayed or not, He knew all that I was going through, and He would have the final verdict.

When court came in session, my wife's cousin took her place back on the stand. My attorney began to cross examine her testimony. He began to ask her questions about that night, that she had not mentioned while being questioned by the DA. Questions about her drinking. "I had a few drinks, maybe 2 or 3. But I wasn't drunk. I wasn't even buzzed." She was asked if she thought she was ok to drive that night. "I wasn't drunk. I was ok to drive. I didn't feel safe in my cousin's home. They started arguing, and I felt it would be better if we left." My attorney again asked if she

THOUGHT IT WOULD BE A GOOD IDEA FOR HER TO DRIVE, KNOWING THAT SHE HAD BEEN DRINKING, AND SHE WOULD HAVE HAD AN 8 MONTH OLD BABY IN THE CAR. "YES. I WAS FINE. I COULD HAVE DROVE. I ONLY HAD 3 BEERS AT THE MOST. BUT I DON'T REMEMBER." MY ATTORNEY QUESTIONED THE FACT OF WHY MY WIFE AND I WERE ARGUING IN THE FIRST PLACE. AND ASKED HER TO DESCRIBE WHAT HAPPENED WHEN SHE TRIED TO GRAB THE BABY. "WELL WE WERE GOING TO GO TO MY STEP BROTHER'S HOUSE, BUT HE WOULDN'T LET HER. SO THEY WERE ARGUING ABOUT IT. THE BABY WAS SITTING ON THE BED, AND I WAS GOING TO GRAB HER, BUT HE PUSHED HER BACK ON THE BED. THAT'S WHEN HE STARTED CURSING AT ME AND HIT ME." SHE ADDED THE LAST PART FOR DRAMATIC EFFECT. MY ATTORNEY READ THE POLICE REPORT TO HER. THE COURTROOM LISTENED AS MY ATTORNEY READ THE DIFFERENT VERSION SHE HAD MADE IN HER POLICE REPORT. "IT SAYS HERE THAT YOU GRABBED THEIR DAUGHTER OFF OF THE BED, AND THEN THE DEFENDANT TOOK HER FROM YOU AND PLACED HER ON THE BED. ISN'T THAT WHAT YOU INITIALLY TOLD THE POLICE? BUT NOW YOU ARE TRYING TO MAKE IT SEEM AS IF MY CLIENT THREW HIS DAUGHTER ON THE BED, AND YOU NEVER GRABBED HER." MY ATTORNEY HAD SHED LIGHT ON THE DIFFERENCE IN TESTIMONY. BUT SHE COULDN'T REMEMBER IF SHE SAID THAT. "I DON'T KNOW WHY I TOLD THE POLICE THAT." MY ATTORNEY CONTINUED READING ALOUD, AND ASKED WHY SHE HAD NEVER MENTIONED IN HER ENTIRE REPORT THAT SHE HAD BEEN DRINKING ALCOHOL. BUT SHE SAID BECAUSE SHE WAS NEVER ASKED. HE ASKED HER IF SHE HAD ANY CHILDREN. AND IF SHE THOUGHT IT WOULD BE OK FOR HER CHILD TO RIDE IN A CAR WITH A DRUNK DRIVER. "IT WOULD NOT BE OK. BUT I WASN'T DRUNK." MY ATTORNEY TRIED TO MAKE IT CLEAR TO THE JURY, WHY ME AND MY WIFE WERE ARGUING. HE DESCRIBED A FATHER CONCERNED FOR HIS CHILD'S SAFETY, AND THE INSISTING OF AN INTOXICATED FEMALE TO THE CHILD'S MOTHER, PERSISTING FOR THEM TO LEAVE AGAINST THE FATHER'S WISHES. "I WASN'T EVEN BUZZED. I DIDN'T FEEL MY COUSIN SHOULD HAVE TO STAY THERE, JUST BECAUSE HE WANTED HER TO STAY THERE. I WAS OK TO DRIVE." MY ATTORNEY PROCEEDED TO ASK ABOUT THE HIT TO THE HEAD. HE ASKED WHY SHE COULDN'T REMEMBER WHAT PART OF HER HEAD SHE WAS HIT, OR BY WHICH HAND she was struck. "It was so fast and unexpected that I didn't really notice, until my head was throbbing. That's when I knew I had been hit. But I don't know how or where. But it hurt really bad." She described a flash slap to the top of her head, from an unexplainable angle. She couldn't remember which side of her head was struck, or which hand I might have used... It had happened so fast she said. That's about as fast as lightning. Under different circumstances, I might have taken pride in that kind of ability. But I was far from flattered by her remarks. I couldn't believe her false accusation. That alone was enough to convict me for battery... But then the ultimate gory of being chocked half to death was icing on the cake. Stick a fork in it, I was done. I couldn't possibly beat that. My attorney asked her to describe how the phone was knocked out of her hand, and why she didn't know who had knocked it out of her hand. "In your police report you claim that the defendant grabbed the phone from your hand. But now you're saying that someone knocked it from your hand. But you don't remember who. Why is that? Why are you giving this courtroom a different version today?" My attorney was doing a great job of cross examining her testimony. I was quite satisfied by his defense on my case. I started to feel a bit more hopeful. He was making her testimony lose solidarity. She had obviously changed her story from the one she gave the police on the night of the incident. "Well I don't remember what I told the police that night. But I'm telling the truth. Someone hit my hand, but I can't remember who. My back was facing them. So it could have been the defendant, but I'm not sure." She didn't remember why she gave the police a totally different version, but she swore that what she was saying was true. My attorney continued his questioning, and began to ask about the part where she says that I choked her. "You say that he choked you. He choked you so hard that you blacked out. Now we all seen how difficult it was for you to relive that memory. But can you describe how you were choked?" He asks her to give details, and even brings in a drawing board for her to use. He asked her to draw on the board, and to point out the living room and the position of everyone who was there when the incident took place. She drew a diagram and began to explain what took place. "I had my purse over my shoulder and my phone in my hand. I was going to call the police and my phone got knocked out of my hand. It hit the ground and the back part of the phone fell off. The battery was lying next to the phone. When I turned around he was standing in front of me. He grabbed me, and spun me around into a weird position. I'm not sure how to describe it. But he was choking me, and dragging me towards the stairs at the same time." My attorney stopped her to get more specifics. He asked her to describe which way her body was facing, and which way my body was facing. "He was facing away from the stairs, and I was facing towards the stairs." She tells my attorney. My attorney adds, "So he was facing away from the stairs while he was choking you? So in order for him to drag you towards the stairs, he would have to be walking backwards. Does this seem very likely for my defendant to be capable to do this? How much do you weigh?" My attorney got her weight and made a quick comparison to my build. He was not convinced that her description to being choked made much sense. He asked her to finish her version of what happened. "Well I was in a weird choking position, and I passed out. I remember blacking out, and that was the last thing I remember. When I woke up I was confused. He was standing over me, hitting me. I was lying on the ground and his cousin was pulling him off of me. I didn't know what was going on. I thought I was in a dream. I saw them run down the stairs, and they left. After they left, I was looking for my purse so that I could leave, but it was gone." My attorney asked her if she saw me take her purse. "No I did not. But when they left I told my cousin my purse was missing. And she called him about it. She asked him if he had my purse, but he told her he didn't." Her testimony was very brutal. She had described herself as being attacked and choked half to death. It hadn't even made any sense. She had made herself an innocent victim of a senseless crime. The picture she painted was that of a violent attack against an innocent bystander. As I sat there looking like the scum of the earth... I had been slandered to the point of my defeat. My attorney made his final argument to her testimony. "In your report you claim he stole your purse. But today you say that you never saw him take your purse. Why do you believe he stole your purse? Did you ever see him with your purse?" She was unable to give a solid answer to my lawyer's questions. Only that she assumed I took her purse. She was excused from the stand, but her testimony had left its mark. Court was adjourned for the day.

# THIRTY TWO

The prosecutor had based his case on the single witness testimony of my wife's cousin. He had no further witnesses. My attorney now had his chance to call witnesses on my behalf, to defend my innocence. The first witness called was my wife. She entered the court room dressed elegantly in heels and a dress. She was looking very lovely. I hadn't seen her for some time, and I was taken by her beauty. She placed her hand on the Bible, and made an oath to tell the truth. I could tell she was nervous, because I knew she got anxious when she had to speak in front of a large group. My attorney respectfully welcomed her to the courtroom, and began his array of questioning. He started from the beginning. From the day that her cousin had first came to our home to visit... Which, was actually her home, since I wasn't allowed to live there anymore. He began to bring out hidden aspects that her cousin wasn't revealing. "My cousin didn't get along with my husband. She thinks he's not good for me. She's used to telling her boyfriends what to do, and she's not used to having a guy tell her what to do. So when she sees how my husband doesn't let me do certain things, she gets upset. She thinks he's controlling. But she doesn't realize that he's just looking out for me and the baby. That night, she wanted me to go with her to go see some guy she's talking to. She didn't want to go alone. I knew that my husband wasn't going to allow that, but she kept insisting for me to go. So when my husband told me it was too late for me and the baby to go anywhere, she flipped out." My wife described her cousin better than I ever could. I didn't even know the girl. I had met her that weekend for the first time, and didn't know anything about her. Other than, the fact that she had a daughter by a guy that she was no longer with. My wife also had exposed the fact that they were going to go to some guy's house. I had been under the impression that they were going to go back to her cousin's house that night. I couldn't believe my wife had lied to me. I would have never allowed her to go to some guy's house at 3 in the morning... That's for sure. My wife knew that wasn't going to happen. And now it made more sense, as to why her cousin had reacted the way that she had that night. My attorney asked my wife what she meant by flipping out. "Well she started to argue with my husband. And my husband told her to mind her own business. When he told her that she got more upset, and started talking crazy to him and pointing in his face. Then out of no where she picked up our daughter. It all happened so fast, I had no idea she was going to do that. I'm not sure what she was thinking, or what she was going to do, but I got worried for a minute. But my husband took her from my cousin and put her back on the bed. I could tell my cousin was drunk. She was acting different." My wife helped clear up the part where her cousin was claiming that I pushed my daughter onto the bed. My attorney asked for her to repeat that last part. He wanted to make it clear, and contrast her cousin's testimony. "So you say he took her from you cousin? How exactly did he do that? Was the baby hurt in any way? You say that your cousin seemed drunk. Can you explain why you thought she was drunk?" My wife described again how I took my daughter from her cousin, and made it clear that my daughter was not hurt in any way. "The baby was fine. She was just lying there. I could tell my cousin was drunk because she got all emotional. When my husband was yelling at her, she started to cry. She wasn't being normal." My wife described the effects the alcohol was making her cousin feel. She had grown up with her cousin, and they had gotten drunk together in the past. She knew her cousin better than anyone else in the courtroom. And my wife admitted that everyone in the house was feeling the effects of alcohol... Even my wife. My wife's testimony proceeded and she began to describe what happened next. "My cousin and my husband's cousin went to the living room to talk. While they were in there, she called the cops but hung up. My husband's cousin came back to the room to tell us, and my husband got very upset. I was upset with her also. She was trying to cause problems for my family. I wanted her to leave. My husband and her started arguing. She started to get in his face. She was talking back to him, and pointing in his face. My husband tried to grab her arms and pin them to her sides. He had her in like a bear hug, but she was resisting." My attorney asked for specific details. He made sure that she described what her cousin was doing to invoke the restraint. After she made her best attempt to describe what had happened, my attorney let the DA cross examine her... I was beginning to feel a bit more confident. My wife's testimony had shed truth to the detestable lies of her cousin.

The prosecutor's approach was harsh. His questions were accusatory. He focused extensively on her relationship with me. He brought up the fact that my wife and I had an open CPS case. He wanted to know why I was not allowed to live in the home. He was insinuating that I was court ordered not to have any contact with my wife and daughter. He was winning points in his favor, by putting my character down. No juror would sympathize with a "child abuser"... After all, everyone's perception of CPS is to protect a child from abusive parents, even though this was not the reality of our CPS case. But we live in a brain washed society, manipulated by the media. And we judge based on stereotypes and prejudices. So the admittance of the CPS case, strongly hurt my credibility. My wife became very nervous... The DA's tone was intimidating her. Her anxiety started to kick in... I could tell because her answers were beginning to delay, and she would ask for the prosecutor to repeat the questions. She even became embarrassed at not understanding some of his questions. The DA became upset with her and began yelling at her and demanding answers. My wife was so distraught, that my lawyer requested a recess. "Judge can you give the court a short recess. We've been in court almost 2 hours. My witness has been given many questions. I think we should take a short break." The judge ordered a short recess. I was pissed at the prosecutor for being so harsh with my wife. I felt bad for her. The DA was being so disrespectful towards her, that he was making her feel bad. I could see my wife was holding back tears. It was not her fault for not being able to understand his questions, or remember every detail of every question. My wife suffers from a disability. This jerk (the prosecutor) obviously didn't understand that. Even though she had mentioned it to him, when he asked her why CPS had felt a need to make a case against us. I asked my lawyer to tell the prosecutor to show some respect. "Tell him to stop harassing her. He's making her uncomfortable. He's six foot two, and she's only a female. He needs to stop intimidating her. She can't even answer his questions because she's so nervous. She has a learning disability. Doesn't he understand that? What is he, an idiot?" My attorney agreed to talk to the prosecutor. The DA was treating my wife like some piece of crap... I was hoping the jury was seeing the abuse my wife was taking. Hopefully this would hurt his prosecution. On the other hand, I was sure they were getting as annoyed as I was, at my wife's constant "Can you repeat the question". It was delaying the whole process. Everyone just wanted this thing to be over with, so that everyone could go on with their lives. No one wants to be in court, or have to do jury duty. And my wife was so nervous that she couldn't even understand simple questions. The prosecutor was extremely annoyed with

HER, BUT THAT WAS NO RIGHT TO INTIMIDATE AND BELITTLE HER. WHAT KIND OF PROFESSIONAL, LAW REPRESENTING OFFICIAL, BEHAVES IN THIS FORM? IT'S DEGRADING TO THE PROFESSION... AND VERY UNAPPEALING. LOW CLASS MIGHT APPLY.

MY WIFE TOOK HER PLACE BACK ON THE WITNESS STAND. I NOTICED HER CHANGE IN ATTITUDE. HER ANSWERS HELD CONTEMPT FOR THE DA. I BEGAN TO HOPE SHE DIDN'T MAKE HERSELF LOOK BAD. SHE WAS BEGINNING TO HURT MY CHANCES AT BEATING THE CASE. MY FEELINGS OF CONFIDENCE HAD QUICKLY DISAPPEARED. I WAS NOW FACED WITH THE STRONG POSSIBILITY OF GOING TO JAIL. MY WIFE WAS STILL ANSWERING QUESTIONS, BUT SHE WAS GIVING SHORT AND SOMETIMES AWKWARD RESPONSES. BY THE TIME SHE WAS DONE BEING INTERROGATED, I WAS LEFT WITH LITTLE HOPE. THE JUDGE EXCUSED HER, AND SHE QUIETLY LEFT THE COURTROOM. I WATCHED AS MY LOVELY WIFE EXITED. MY ATTORNEY WOULD CALL HIS NEXT WITNESS. "I WOULD LIKE TO CALL IN THE REPORTING OFFICER TO THE STAND." MY ATTORNEY CALLED IN THE POLICE OFFICER WHO TOOK MY WIFE'S COUSIN'S REPORT. SHE HAD BEEN THE OFFICER WHO CONDUCTED THE INVESTIGATION AND DID THE REPORT. MY ATTORNEY WANTED TO CLARIFY THE DISCREPANCIES BETWEEN THE POLICE REPORT AND THE TESTIMONY GIVEN BY MY WIFE'S COUSIN. THEY WERE VERY CONTRADICTING, AND MY ATTORNEY NEEDED TO MAKE THIS CLEAR TO THE JURY. IT WAS OBVIOUS MY ACCUSER WAS LYING. HE WOULD QUESTION THE POLICE OFFICER ABOUT THAT NIGHT. "HOW LONG HAVE YOU BEEN WORKING AS A DETECTIVE? WHEN YOU DO AN INVESTIGATION, IS IT COMMON TO ASK IF DRUGS OR ALCOHOL WAS INVOLVED?" MY ATTORNEY BEGINS. SHE ESTABLISHES HER CREDIBILITY AS AN OFFICER, AND HER QUALIFICATIONS IN DEALING WITH INVESTIGATIONS. SHE ANSWERS "YES IT IS A QUESTION WE GENERALLY ASK." MY ATTORNEY HAD ASKED MY WIFE'S COUSIN WHY SHE HADN'T MENTIONED SHE HAD BEEN DRINKING ALCOHOL, AND HER RESPONSE WAS THAT SHE WAS NEVER ASKED. BUT IT SEEMED THE POLICE OFFICER GENERALLY ASKS THAT SORT OF QUESTION. SO SHE WAS OBVIOUSLY CONCEALING THE FACT THAT SHE HAD BEEN DRINKING FROM THE POLICE OFFICER. MY ATTORNEY FOLLOWED UP WITH ANOTHER QUESTION, AS TO WHY THAT WAS A NECESSARY QUESTION WHEN MAKING A report. "Well if drugs or alcohol were involved it can become a factor in determining whether the perception of the complaining victim is accurate or not. It can also give a better understanding as to why someone might have behaved the way they did, if they were under the influence of a drug or alcohol." My attorney asked if the police officer had asked the complaining victim, if she had been drinking that night. "I believe I did. It should be in my report." My attorney asks her if she has had a chance to go over the report. To which she said she had. He then asked why it was not in her report that the complaining victim had been drinking that night. "I'm not sure. I don't think she told me that she had been drinking. If she had told me, it would be in my report." After my attorney got this out of her, I became impressed at his ability to bring forth facts. He was defending me very well, and I was thankful. He continued to the part about where she states that I hit her on the top of her head. He asks if there were any photos taken. "Yes. We took many photos. I'm sure you have been given copies." My attorney brings out photos that were taken from that night. He asks if there were any taken that showed the top of her head. "I don't remember. What ever pictures we took, you should have." My attorney agrees. And he explains that there were none taken to show the top of her head. The pictures that were admitted into evidence, were pictures from the side view, pictures under her jaw line, and pictures of the inside of her mouth. But none were taken from the top of her head. "Why is that? If she is stating that the defendant struck her on the top of her head, and in her testimony she gave before the jury, she described it as a hard blow to the head, why was there not any pictures taken? It seems rather incongruous don't you think?" The officer had no valid answer. She did not know why there were no pictures taken for the top of her head. He then asked her about the pictures that were in evidence. He asked her to describe what each picture showed. "In this picture you can see a bruise by her chin along her jaw line. And in these pictures you can see redness along the gum line. Possibly her braces cut the inside of her mouth." Four pictures were taken into evidence. The jury was shown the over sized photos. I was shocked by the bruise on her cheek. I didn't understand how she had got that. I started to wonder if I had actually hurt her during my forceful eviction. The picture of her gum line was over exaggerated. The redness looked like bad gingivitis, and showed no cuts whatsoever. Another picture showed bad acne. The only really incriminating photo was the picture with the bruise. I couldn't believe she had gotten bruised... This was going to be an open and shut case. My only defense now was to show meaningful self defense. But that would be difficult considering the fact that she is a female. The law that protects a person from evicting someone from their home, didn't apply to me since I was no longer on the lease. I had responded as the owner of the home, by kicking her out, but I was not acting under the law, because I was basically just a guest in someone else's home. I had no legal defense to what I had done... I was powerless. My attorney asked her if the complaining victim had to be seen by a doctor after the incident, or if she went to the hospital. The police officer stated that my wife's cousin did not need to be seen by a medical doctor, and that she hadn't gone to the hospital to treat any of her injuries. After questioning from both sides, the police officer was excused. Another long day in court had gone by, and court would adjourn until the following day... I would have to wait and see what would happen.

# THIRTY THREE

This would be the final day. The jury would listen to one last witness, and then they would decide my ultimate fate. My attorney called in one of my cousins from that night. He had been at the house during that night, but had left early with his female friend. He took his place on the stand. His testimony would hopefully help my case. Things didn't seem too hopeful. My attorney asked him several questions about that night. He asked him about things we did that night. He asked if he had seen anything unusual that night. "Not really. My cousin and his wife seemed to not be getting along at the time. They had some sort of disagreement between themselves." My attorney asked on a scale from one to ten, how bad the disagreement was. My cousin quickly responded with "one", before my attorney had gotten a chance to finish the question. The judge rebuked him for speaking out of turn. The judge explained that the court reporter needed everyone to speak one at a time, so that she could type what was being said. My cousin apologized, and explained that he had been waiting in the lobby for the past few days waiting to get his testimony over with. He was anxious to get this over with... I didn't blame him. I felt bad for putting him through this. He gained empathy with a few of the jurors, but his attitude came off as rude. His answers were rushed and undescriptive. My attorney felt my cousin's frustration, and hurried his questions. He cut to the point. "After you left, what happened the next morning?" My attorney asked. My cousin explained that I arrived at his friend's house where he was staying. And he told the court that he noticed blood on my shirt, and a deep gash on my arm. "Can you describe how much blood? Was his shirt soaked or was it just drops of blood? Did the cut look like it could have been caused by a scratch?" The prosecutor objected. He did not see how this was relevant to the charges. Since, my cousin had not witnessed the events, and the gash to my arm had not been entered into any evidence. The prosecutor was granted his objection, and my cousin's final remarks concerning the gash were excluded from his testimony... He was then excused. My attorney had been hoping to factor in an act of self defense. The gash to my arm had been caused during my altercation with my wife's cousin. I think she may have scratched me. But it was not going to be admissible, and I would have to lay primarily on my wife's testimony, as well as the police officers contradicting report. The prosecutor was then given a chance to give his closing argument. He spent nearly an hour attacking my character, and making me seem like the worst of the worst. He praised the complaining victim, and placed her on a pedestal. He said she was a hero... A hero for being brave, enough to come to court and face her attacker. He didn't mention the fact that it was he, the prosecutor, who was pressing charges, and not my wife's cousin. She had been subpoenaed to court. If she hadn't shown up she could have faced charges herself, and possibly been arrested. It was ingenious for him to portray her as mother Mary herself. When my attorney finally had a chance to give his closing statement, everyone had been won over by the DA's extensive closing argument. I was eager for my attorney to speak in my defense. My attorney broke down the events in the trial, and explained all of the facts that were admitted. He gave a long description of my side of the coin, and the situation I was in. I was being accused by a woman that I had barely even met. And she didn't like me even before she met me. He explained how the effects of alcohol had

PLAYED A PART IN THIS UNFORTUNATE INCIDENT, BUT THAT THE REAL VICTIM WAS ME... I HAD TO BE THE ONE PRESENT TO COURT EVERYDAY. I HAD TO BE THE ONE FACING MY ACCUSER, AND SUFFERING THE HUMILIATION OF BEING ACCUSED OF THINGS I HADN'T DONE. HE DESCRIBED MY SIDE OF THE COIN SO WELL, THAT IT GAVE ME GOOSE BUMPS. I FELT EXPOSED TO THE ENTIRE COURTROOM, AND I WAS EMBARRASSED. AFTER HE FINISHED HIS CLOSING ARGUMENT, HE LEFT THE JURY WITH THE TASK OF MAKING THE DECISION THAT WOULD AFFECT THE REST OF MY LIFE. THE JURY HELD MY FATE... BUT I WAS IN GOD'S HANDS.

AFTER ONLY AN HOUR THE JURY HAD FOUND THEIR VERDICT... "FOR COUNT ONE, THE CRIME OF BATTERY, WE THE JURY FIND THE DEFENDANT GUILTY. AS FOR COUNT TWO, THE CRIME OF PETTY THEFT, WE THE JURY FIND THE DEFENDANT NOT GUILTY." I WAS SHOCKED... AND VERY DISAPPOINTED. I WAS HOPING THE JURY WOULD FIND MY WIFE'S COUSIN'S TESTIMONY INADMISSIBLE AND DISREGARD IT. SHE HAD OBVIOUSLY LIED. THAT SHOULD HAVE BEEN ENOUGH TO FIND PROBABLE DOUBT. BUT I GUESS THE JURY FELT SYMPATHY FOR THE FEMALE, AND HAD DECIDED TO CONVICT ME... I WASN'T THAT SURPRISED. I HAD JUST HOPED TO BE REDEEMED FROM ALL THE LIES. I WAS GOING TO BE REMANDED AND TAKEN INTO CUSTODY. THE JUDGE WAITED FOR THE JURY TO BE EXCUSED. HE DID NOT WANT THEM TO WITNESS WHAT WOULD HAPPEN NEXT, AFTER THEIR VERDICT HAD BEEN MADE. THIS WAS TO SPARE THE JURY OF ANY GUILT IN CAUSING MY PUNISHMENT. THE BAILIFF APPROACHED ME AFTER THE JURY LEFT, AND PLACED ME IN HANDCUFFS. I WAS THEN ESCORTED INTO THE HOLDING CELL WITH THE OTHER INMATES. I WAS TO BE SENTENCED THE FOLLOWING WEEK. I COULDN'T BELIEVE I WAS BACK IN JAIL. I GUESS THIS WAS WHERE I NEEDED TO BE. GOD HAD ALLOWED ME TO GO TO JAIL ONCE AGAIN... I DIDN'T RESIST THE FEELING, OR COMPLAIN. I WAS WILLING TO ACCEPT MY PUNISHMENT FROM GOD FOR WHAT I HAD DONE. THE ALTERCATION HAD NOT HAPPENED THE WAY MY WIFE'S COUSIN HAD SAID IT HAD, BUT I WAS WILLING TO FACE THE CONSEQUENCES. AS LONG AS GOD KNEW IN MY HEART I WAS SORRY FOR what I had done, that was all that mattered. After all is said and done, "Only God can judge me".

## THIRTY FOUR

A WEEK HAD PASSED, AND I HAD BEEN DEALING WITH MY CONVICTION FAIRLY WELL. I WAS TAKING ADVANTAGE OF THE OPPORTUNITY TO HAVE FREE HOUSING AND FOOD. I WAS TIRED OF BEING HOMELESS, AND NOT KNOWING WHERE I WOULD BE SLEEPING EVERY NIGHT. HERE I WAS GUARANTEED A BED, FOOD, AND A SHOWER EVERY DAY. IT WAS RELAXING, AND I BEGAN TO USE THE TIME TO REFLECT ON ALL THAT HAD HAPPENED. I HAD DECIDED I WOULD WRITE A STORY ABOUT ALL THAT I HAD WENT THROUGH IN THE PAST YEAR. IT HAD BEEN SUCH A LONG AND CRAZY EXPERIENCE. I BRUSHED MY TEETH, SHAVED, AND GOT IN LINE TO GO TO COURT. THE PROCESS FOR GOING TO COURT WAS VERY HECTIC. HUNDREDS OF INMATES BEING PLACED IN SEPARATE HOLDING TANKS FOR HOURS, WAITING TO CATCH A BUS, WAS VERY EXHAUSTING... AND AGGRAVATING. BUT THE BUS RIDE ITSELF WAS SOMEWHAT PLEASANT. I GOT A CHANCE TO BREATHE FRESH AIR, AND ENJOY THE VIEW. I HAD GOTTEN SO CAUGHT UP IN MY NEW SURROUNDINGS, THAT THE OUTSIDE WORLD SEEMED LIKE A DISTANT MEMORY. JAIL WAS BEGINNING TO GROW ON ME. WHEN I GOT TO THE COURTHOUSE, I WAS PLACED IN ANOTHER HOLDING TANK. I WAS GIVEN A CHANCE TO SPEAK TO MY ATTORNEY BEFORE COURT. HE TOLD ME THAT THE DA WAS ASKING FOR THE MAXIMUM SENTENCE OF 6 MONTHS... I WAS IN DISBELIEF. THE OFFERED PLEA AGREEMENT, THAT I HAD REFUSED BEFORE TRIAL HAD BEGUN, HAD BEEN 30 DAYS IN CUSTODY. THIS WAS WAY MORE THEN THE PLEA DEAL. I WAS BEING PUNISHED FOR USING MY RIGHT TO A JURY TRIAL... THIS WASN'T VERY PALATABLE. MY ATTORNEY WOULD TRY TO GET IT REDUCED TO MAYBE 60 DAYS, BUT IT WAS going to be difficult. We had lost the trial, and the ball was in the prosecutor's court. It was all up to the judge. He also explained that I would probably be ordered to attend anger management classes. But that I wouldn't have to pay the $550 that the prosecutor was alleging for the amount in restitution, since I was found not guilty to the petty theft of her purse. I was not happy with the outcome... But I had no choice. When it was time for my case to be heard, the guard escorted me into the courtroom. The judge listened to the DA's request for me to serve 120 days in jail. Uttering that I was a threat to the public, and that I needed to remain in jail until I learned my lesson. He stated that his initial request had been for me to serve the maximum 180 days in jail, but since he wanted me to do anger management classes upon my release, he had settled on 120 days of jail time. And he also wanted me to pay $550 in restitution fines... My attorney objected. My attorney argued the fact that I had been acquitted on the petty theft charge by the jury, and that it would be unlawful to make me pay for something that I had been found not guilty of. He also brought up the fact that the initial plea bargain had been 30 days county jail, and that I was now being railroaded for using my amendment right to a jury trial. "I ask that my client be given a fair sentence in this case. He would be willing to serve 60 days maximum for this conviction. This charge is a misdemeanor, and my client has shown a great deal of cooperation. Your honor, the jury's ruling did not go in our favor, but he shouldn't have to be punished for exercising his right to a jury trial." As both attorney's made their final arguments, the judge had reached his decision... He sentenced me to 90 days in jail. He also ordered me to attend 26 weeks of anger management on my release. Three years court probation, and $550 in restitution. He had ordered a hearing date to contest the restitution charge, granted in favor of my attorney's request to appeal. I thanked my attorney and shook his hand... I was then taken back into the holding tank.

I spent the next few weeks writing letters, and keeping my mind occupied. I had been sentenced to 3 months in jail. But I would be able to serve only 2 months, if I stayed out of trouble. After a while it wasn't so bad. I tried to remain positive, and waited for God to make something positive out of this whole situation. He can always turn a bad circumstance, into a blessing... It just depends on how you look at things. After about 3 weeks, my name had been called for court. I was confused, and started to think the worse. I suspected maybe the DA was going to pick up the charges from my mother in-law. When I got to the courthouse, and got a chance to speak to my lawyer, I asked him what was going on. He told me that there had been a typo in the protective order from the victim, and they needed to serve me the papers. But that I wouldn't have to go before the judge. "I also have some good news. It seems you won your appeal against CPS. They dropped the case. I thought you might want to know. So when you get out of jail you can be with your family. Congratulations." I was ecstatic! I couldn't believe it... I had won the appeal against CPS! This was great news... I was shocked. I had been long awaiting for this day to come, and now that it had finally happened I was behind bars... Talk about a case of bad luck. I was in a daze for a good hour or two. I kept running the thought through my head, over and over. I was on cloud 9. By the time I returned to the jail, I had planned to call my brother and give him the good news.

"Hey bro guess what? I won my appeal. I'm about to be rich! I'm gonna sue the hell out of them. Haha. I'm finally gonna be able to go home with my family bro. I can go home now, can you believe it? No more restrictions, no more CPS crap, and no more being homeless. I finally won bro! I'm gonna buy you a house out here when I win my million dollar lawsuit. Watch, you're gonna see." My brother was excited for me. He congratulated me on my victory against CPS. I had been telling him for months, that if I won my appeal I would become a millionaire... But he didn't believe me. Only time would tell, and God would decide. As for now I was just happy to be given the freedom to be with my wife and daughter. "Hey bro can you call my wife on three-way? I want her to come visit me. I want to see her and the baby." My brother connected our call and I heard my wife's voice on the other line... "Hey babe. It's me. I needed to call you and let you know that we won our appeal. You don't have to worry about CPS anymore. I want you to come visit me. I want to see you and the baby." I asked my wife if she could come and visit me. I needed her emotional support during my incarceration. I had gone too long without her, and I needed her by my side. She agreed to come and visit. "Yea I heard. My attorney told me yesterday. I'm glad you can finally come home. I want us all to be together. The baby needs you in her life, and its not easy raising her on my own. I need your help too. I'm just glad that this is all over." My wife was just about as exhausted as I was, and we were both relieved to have an end to this nightmare. My wife would come to the next visit... And she offered to send me money on my books. She didn't want me to be starving in jail. My brother would also send me some money. He felt bad that I had to be in jail... When the call was cut off, due to time limitation, I was left with some joy. I knew that things were going to be better when I got out of jail. I looked forward to my release date. In the meantime I decided to write a story, a story that would explain my long battle with CPS, of how CPS ruined a part of my life, and how it nearly ended my life. A story of how CPS tried to destroy my family... But how they didn't succeed. Thanks to my Lord and savior, Jesus Christ. I realized that God had allowed me to go through such a horrible experience, and had brought me out in VICTORY. My enemies did not succeed in their evil and wicked schemes. When I had lost hope, and thought that there was nothing I could do... I was right. There was nothing I could do. But God could. He did the impossible for me. He did what I couldn't do, and I decided I would share my testimony. Because this is God's testimony. This victory is for God's glory. And there is hope in God. God is bigger than any circumstance or problem. And if you believe in Him, and place your problems in His hands, and let Him do the fighting for you, He will bring you out victorious. I hope this story serves as a blessing. God bless you, and sincerely, "Thank you Lord"... Amen.

Contend, O Lord, with those who contend with me;
fight against those who fight against me.
Take up shield and buckler;
arise and come to my aid.
Brandish spear and javelin
against those who pursue me.
Say to my soul,
"I am your salvation."
May those who seek my life
be disgraced and put to shame;
may those who plot my ruin
be turned back in dismay.
May they be like chaff before the wind,
with the angel of the Lord driving them away;
may their path be dark and slippery,
with the angel of the Lord pursuing them.
Since they hid their net for me without cause
and without cause dig a pit for me,
may ruin overtake them by surprise—
may the net they hid entangle them,
may they fall into the pit, to their ruin.
Then my soul will rejoice in the Lord
and delight in his salvation.
My whole being will exclaim,
"Who is like you, O Lord?
You rescue the poor from those too strong for them,
the poor and needy from those who rob them." —Psalms 35:1–10

www.ingramcontent.com/pod-product-compliance
Lightning Source LLC
Chambersburg PA
CBHW071152290526
45788CB00001BA/447

* 9 7 8 1 4 5 1 5 5 0 7 5 7 *